SIMPLE
PAPER FLOWERS

SIMPLE PAPER FLOWERS

PAULA MILNER

THE GUILD OF MASTER CRAFTSMAN PUBLICATIONS

Contents

Introduction

As children, we are actively encouraged to be creative. We are often pushed to paint, to stick, to draw, to be expressive. A child who is drawing may ask, 'Can I colour the grass red and purple?' The adult replies, 'Of course, why not! You are expressing your creativity!' There are no rules. However, as adults, we worry about how things will look; we want things to be 'perfect'. We 'cannot' paint the grass red. It is green. But we should ask ourselves, 'Why not?'

As adults, we make less time for craft. We WANT to be crafty, we WANT to try and have the time. But, sometimes, craft can feel like a club. If you're 'not particularly crafty', how do you join in? Where do you begin? You want to do 'something', but you don't know who – or maybe even what – to ask. You may not know what craft you even want to do, but you want to try. Maybe the instructions feel too confusing, too overwhelming.

Well, here we are. And here is the deal...

Firstly, we need to make some time. Grab a cuppa and let's sit for half an hour – just us – making flowers. Secondly, we need to embrace our inner crafty child. And finally, there is no cliquey club. We need to just have fun. There are no rules! My objective in this book is to inspire you, to offer a guiding hand to help you get creative. Let's think of it as a simple crafty hug.

I would like to think that these paper flower projects are beautiful, but also that they are realistically accessible. While, of course, we would like a paper buttercup to look EXACTLY like a real buttercup, it is also about enjoying the process of making. I have studied each flower construction to truly understand how they can be recreated in paper form – but without them being so hyper-realistic that they are complex and off-putting. They are simple, but they are not so 'simple' that they are just 'easy'. These projects are meant to feel approachable but also rewarding.

Simple Paper Flowers hopefully strikes that balance between learning new skills but also having the freedom to experiment. While each flower may not always be absolutely 100 per cent botanically correct, I can promise that each bloom does at least feel like the flower or leaf in mind. I have always said that I believe all craft should be two things: fun and achievable. These floral projects are designed for you to simply enjoy creating!

Going back to 'no rules'... Well, this is especially true in the beauty of paper flower making. You don't have to wait for spring to have daffodils. You can have a Christmassy poinsettia all year round. If you want to mix and match blooms from across the seasons, you can! 'Real' poppies last for very little time in a vase, whereas these paper versions can last forever!

There are also no rules to making exactly as I have instructed. I will guide you through the simple techniques and provide advice with measurements, but feel free to change them, even to go beyond them. Utilize the ideas for other blooms, make things twice as big, make small, make lots, change the colours – as long as you enjoy what you are making, you can do whatever you like! Want to make blue daffodils?

Go for it.

About me

I have been crafty pretty much forever. I can remember taking my pocket money to an incredible small independent craft shop and getting excited about beads, and threads, modelling clay, fabrics, paint, paper. And very delightedly for me, I was actively encouraged, in fact, championed to get creative! Not just as a child but long into my teenage years and onwards. Into school, college and onto a First Class BA (Hons) degree at Loughborough University in Printed Textile Design.

My life after university led naturally into the more corporate world, where I was successful, but I craved creativity beyond the office walls. In 2015, I quit my nine-to-five job to establish 'The Crafty Lass' – and that is how my life, as it is now, began. I dreamed of teaching adults, making them see how craft can calm the soul and bring out some of that inner child. How it can offer new skills, moments of quiet reflection, satisfaction and pride. Paper flower making was one of the first crafts I approached with a plan to teach.

While I quickly established myself in a huge variety of crafts, I always found inspiration in nature, flowers, the seasons. I feel immersing ourselves in our natural world can bring many small moments of joy. A walk in the forest, buds emerging, those first spring shoots growing, colourful fresh flowers in a vase. I like to draw nature – most of my fabric designs and ranges are drawn from our natural world.

I found my heart in paper flowers, finding it absolutely fascinating, and delightfully satisfying, that you can turn flat paper – very quickly, simply – into something three-dimensional and joyous! I discovered that I can (and you can, too!) transform basic printer paper into delightful daisies and mould floristry crepe paper into huge peonies or tiny narcissus. You can create prickly holly, or soft and fluttering sunflowers. All you need is paper with just a few additional materials, some sharp scissors and a few crafty magic techniques to get you going. I can't wait to see what you create!

Tools, Materials & Techniques

Tools

Wire Cutters

You will need a strong and sturdy set of steel wire cutters. Some smaller floristry or jewellery-type wire cutters are just too soft to cut through some of the thicker floristry stem wires. Never use scissors to try to cut wire, as this can damage the scissor blades.

Embroidery Scissors

Where needed, these pointy scissors are used to create small holes in woollen felt balls, allowing the stem wire to be glued snugly inside. Alternatively, you can use a sharp tapestry needle.

Paper Scissors

You will need to use a decent pair of sharp paper scissors – any that you feel most comfortable with!

Paintbrush

In this book, a paintbrush is occasionally used for painting PVA glue onto paper to create 'shiny' effects. Any paintbrush will be suitable.

Ruler and Pencil

Both a pencil and ruler will be useful for checking and marking out petal measurements.

Pen

Occasionally, coloured pens are used to add detail to the paper. These can be any felt-tip or fineliner pens in the relevant colour required for the make.

Glue Gun

Alongside paper scissors, a hot glue gun will be the most often used tool throughout this book. Or you can use a cold glue gun version instead, if you prefer. Sometimes, given the small size of the petals, a glue gun can feel quite fiddly. If you feel more comfortable, you can also use a silicone finger protector to help protect your finger from some of the high temperatures of a hot glue gun.

Materials

Floristry Crepe Paper

You will find that floristry crepe paper comes in a huge variety of colours, paper weights and lengths. Unlike standard crepe paper, floristry crepe has a much greater ability to flex, stretch and mould.

In each project, I first focus on what colour you will need or might wish to consider. I have added the recommended colour paper completely as a guide – you are, of course, welcome to go wild and change any of them! You will see throughout this book that I am personally very inspired by colour combinations. I often make the same flower with multiple colour varieties – perhaps with a calming, neutral tonal look or an absolute rainbow riot of colour.

Once you have selected the colour(s), look at the 'weight' of the paper. This will often be listed in grams as a 'gsm' (grams per square metre) number or sometimes by pounds. The higher the number, the greater the weight or thickness of paper. For most of these projects, the weight of floristry crepe paper does not matter – just use whatever you have. However, where I think it ideally needs to be finer or thicker weight, I have specified.

Floristry crepe paper can reeeeeally stretch! With this in mind, you will need to take into consideration the direction of the paper grain to allow you to mould the petals. More often than not, the grain will need to run up the height of the petals and leaves.

Some floristry crepe paper is very smooth, but other varieties have manufacturing or 'machine' lines running indented through them. Where possible, try to make the petals around these machine lines. This sometimes just isn't possible, but it is more effective to not include them.

You could reverse the colours, make the leaves multicoloured and the flower green! Or, make the petals in several colours within the same stem. You can really get creative by going beyond the traditional or expected colours.

Another option is to use 'ombre' floristry crepe paper. This allows you to create a very natural effect with multiple colours within the same flower, such as in the Persian buttercup project.

Paper

In addition to crepe paper, some of the projects are made from standard papers and cardstock – even basic printer paper! As already mentioned, where necessary, I have suggested the ideal weight of the paper – but try not to worry too much about this detail. Choose whatever colour you would like and just enjoy creating.

Don't forget to keep all the little paper scraps. These can often be used for either small petal projects, or saved for crafts such as card making or découpage. Or, if you feel they won't be used – pop the scraps into recycling!

Glues and Tape

The main adhesive used throughout these projects is hot glue. This is a very effective glue that allows you to work quickly: it dries quickly and provides a strong bond between paper layers. In some of the projects, you could use 'red liner' double-sided tape, if you prefer.

The second main type of adhesive used in these projects is floristry crepe tape. This, in my opinion, is magic tape! When you touch the tape, initially, it will feel dry and smooth. However, if you stretch it out, the tacky glue will be revealed from inside! You will need to ensure you stretch it enough when attaching the petals to guarantee there is enough glue to adhere everything together. Sometimes you might think you can attach several petals at once using this tape – but, unfortunately, there might then not be enough glue to hold everything together, meaning the flower head can collapse. The best approach is to use a small amount of tape for every petal. This not only will ensure the flower stays together, it also often will mean you create the natural flower shape at the back of the petals, too. As you are making, if you ever feel like the flower is 'loose', add some extra tape, pulling it really taut to ensure everything really sticks – or you can try to combine it with a glue gun for extra adhesion.

Floristry crepe tape comes in a variety of colours. More often than not, I have suggested to use green for the stems throughout these projects. Sometimes, I recommend a dark or light green will be more suitable, but whatever you have available will work. You can also get floristry crepe tape in a range of brighter colours such as pink, red or even a vibrant turquoise! You can, of course – as with all of these projects – use whatever colour you would like.

PVA glue, which is sometimes referred to as 'school glue', isn't used as an adhesive in these projects. Instead it is used as a glaze to add shine to the paper surface. If you prefer, you can completely skip the steps that use it if you don't have any to hand.

Other Materials

Wire

The wire used in these projects is measured in gauges, which is simply the thickness of the wire. In the majority of projects, the main stem wire is paper-covered floristry stem wire, approximately 16 gauge in weight. If you are unable to get wire at this gauge, feel free to experiment with whatever is available.

Stub Wire

A much finer, often shorter wire, stub wire is sometimes green or silver in colour. We will occasionally use it inside petals to create a further option for moulding the petal shapes. It can also be used as the main stem where necessary, and I have specified when in each project.

In regards to deciding on the length of each main stem wire, I quite often do NOT include one. This is because it simply depends on what you are making the flower for! While some flowers naturally lend themselves to having a full long stem, such as lilies and peonies, if you are planning to include them in a wreath, for example, you may wish the stem to be much shorter. Or, if you are adding a small delicate rose into a huge bouquet, you may want to make the stem much longer to allow for more flexibility in how you incorporate all of the blooms together. Adjust the length to however you feel is best.

Flower Pips

In some of the projects, I have suggested using flower pips, which are sometimes used in floral arrangements to resemble stamens. They are often double sided and can be folded in half to allow you to attach to the stem. They come in a wide variety of colours – use whatever you would like for the required makes.

Air-Dry Clay

Clay is also used in the holly project to make the sphere berry shapes. While you will need only a small amount to create them, in combination with the nail varnish, these materials can really make a difference, creating a very effective and natural appearance.

Woollen Felt Balls

Often used as the centre of flowers, woollen felt balls have a lovely textural quality, and come in various sizes and a wide range of colours. The most common sizes are ⅜in (10mm), $\frac{9}{16}$in (15mm) and ¾in (20mm), and I have specified which ones to use in the relevant projects. You can use small craft pompoms or polystyrene balls instead if desired, but I think woollen felt balls have the right density of both texture and colour for these projects.

Nail Varnish

There is only one project in this book that utilizes nail varnish – holly – for those majestically shiny red berries! You can use paint, or some sort of enamel instead, but nail varnish dries quickly, has that lovely glossy sheen to it and is also readily available! It is helpfully in a small bottle, too, at often very economical prices.

Straws

There is only one project in this book that requires the use of straws – wild primrose – for the very centre. Craft straws often come in larger packs – but they can be used for all sorts of fun craft projects.

Techniques

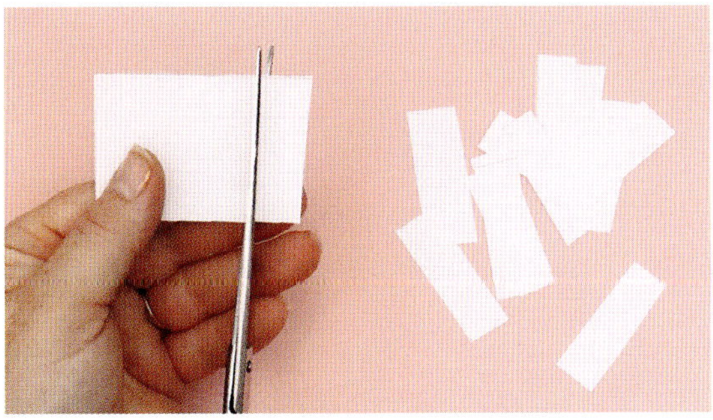

Cutting Rectangles and Squares

I often suggest cutting rectangles or squares before moving on to shaping the petals. This helps to keep the petal sizes consistent, and it also helps to create less waste by ensuring you use only what you need for each flower.

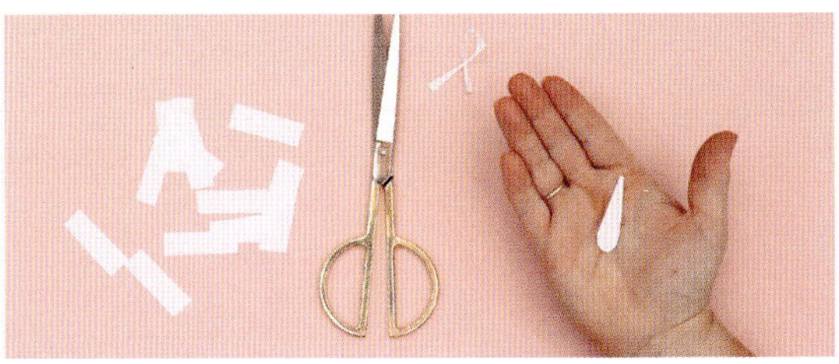

Shaping

For each flower, I try to describe the shape you need to cut out for each petal alongside the photos that will help you to see the outline of each petal. I often refer to objects, such as 'almonds' or 'hot-air balloons', to try to help you comparably visualize what to cut out. Nature isn't always perfect, so it would be good for a little flower character here and there. However, some of the more common shapes I refer to are shown on page 166.

Folding

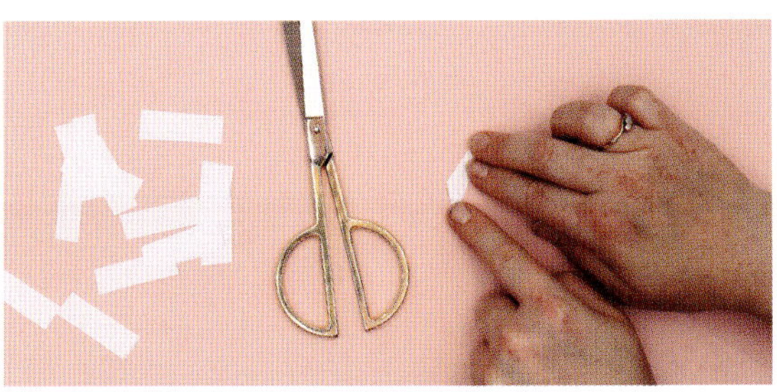

Folding standard paper to create simple creases can quickly and easily add shape and definition to petals.

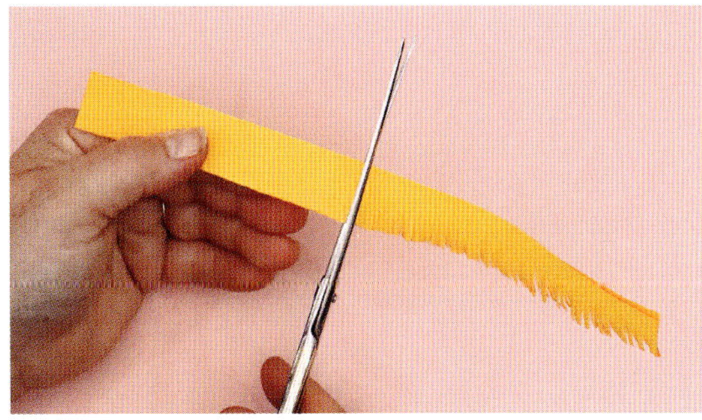

Frilling

Several of the projects call for rectangles that are then cut into to create a frilled effect. I specify measurements in some that are just a few millimetres. As long as they are similarly sized, you don't need to worry too much about exactly how wide each cut is, but ideally cut them as small or as close to my recommendation as you can.

Colouring

In some projects, pens are used to add definition and important details to petals, which can help make them look like the natural flower. Floristry crepe paper will soak up the ink really easily!

Scrunching

Paper can actually be remarkably strong, so be brave with your movements! Screwing up standard paper can add texture – creases and lines that add character to the petals. Screwing up floristry crepe paper can help relax the stiff grain of the papers.

Curving

Gently curving petals can help mimic their natural shape. Use your fingers to gently bend petals into curves, or pull the paper over a pencil or ruler edge.

Using the Grain

Unless otherwise specified, the grain of the crepe paper should run up the height of the initial rectangle. This does vary when making the flower centres.

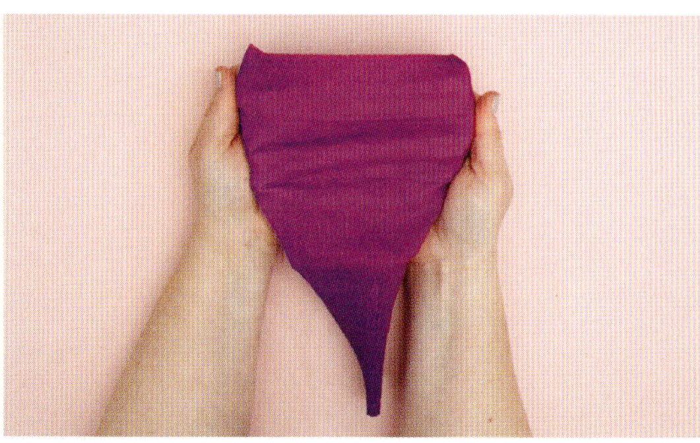

Stretching

Before creating petals, sometimes it is best to completely stretch floristry crepe paper out so that all the textured grain becomes smooth. This is useful when creating very feathery light petals, such as in the daffodil or sunflower projects, since the floristry crepe turns into almost a tissue paper-like quality but is much stronger.

Moulding with Wire

If petals or leaves need additional moulding, it can be useful to incorporate some stub wire inside the flower – it will allow you to bend and shape each petal however you wish – and they will stay exactly how you have shaped them.

Wrapping the Stem

Pull the floristry crepe tape taut as you use and wind it round. This releases the glue contained inside. It is important to ensure you have enough of the glue revealed so that it attaches fully, and the petals are nice and secure.

Adding Sheen with PVA

You can brush PVA glue onto thick paper or card to add a beautiful sheen. Some of these makes, such as the holly and buttercup projects, call for a little bit of preparation upfront. You will need to first apply the PVA glue with a paintbrush and allow it to dry. However, this small additional step can really help to make the petals or leaves have that naturally glossy look. You can also paint PVA glue onto floristry crepe paper – however, it tends to soak in much more and doesn't always create the same sheen effect.

Finishing Touches – Bases (and Leaves)

I have finished each flower by including bases and, where appropriate, foliage. However, if you are making a full bouquet, or perhaps a wreath where the backs will be concealed, you may wish to skip some of these steps – and that is, of course, absolutely fine! But if the flowers will be in a vase and will be seen, it makes sense to complete every flower.

Storage

Exposure to Light

Though paper is pretty hardy, the colours can absolutely be affected by long-term sunlight damage. The dyes within the paper are certainly affected by the natural bleaching caused by sunshine. You may actually embrace this – I often deliberately leave floristry crepe paper in a hot and sunny location to create a natural ombre effect! However, if you want the papers and made flowers to remain perfect, I recommend keeping them away from long-term direct sunlight.

Moisture

Water clearly isn't any paper's friend, and while thicker papers, cards and floristry crepe paper can cope amazingly well with a little dampness, definitely avoid leaving them in moisture dense areas. If you are using the flowers for an event, be aware that marquees hold a LOT of moisture overnight and the flowers can become quite soggy and limp (I say this from experience)! Always store the flowers in a sealed container, or remove them from the environment to provide protection from any overnight dew.

Going Beyond This Book...

Embellishments

Why not experiment even further by adding embellishments to the papers? You could use pens, pencils, crayons, inks, paints... anything you like! Floristry crepe paper can get relatively wet without damaging or tearing. You can spray or paint with a paintbrush directly onto the paper – and leave it to dry on a clean surface. However, don't leave the project to dry on newspaper, because when crepe paper dries, it merges together with the newspaper! Bear in mind that if you add colour to floristry crepe paper surfaces, when you stretch it out the original colour can appear through the grain from underneath – which can make for some really lovely and interesting effects.

You could further decorate the flowers with glitter or buttons. I know some people who have even sprayed their flowers with perfume so they have a lovely smell!

Papers

Standard paper and floristry crepe paper are used for these projects, but you could really experiment with lots of different paper formats – try magazines, newspapers or wrapping paper, or you could upcycle old maps, sheet music or damaged books! You can even make lovely paper flowers from paper cupcake cases.

Other Flowers

While there are lots of lovely blooms within this book, you could easily take these techniques and adapt them to other flowers or leaves. Take a look at the flower you would like to create, and think about what paper would be best suited to replicate its natural petals. Look at the colours, amount of petals and the approximate sizing. Pick and choose the techniques and ideas for whatever you need. The paper flower world, is your oyster...

Happy crafting!

Oxeye Daisy

Leucanthemum vulgare

This is the classic daisy that can often be found in huge abundance adorning country roads. With its bright yellow centre, the oxeye daisy reminds me of a glorious sun surrounded by white fluffy clouds! Made using predominantly simple papers and card, these beautiful daisies would be lovely on their own or coordinated among a big, blousy summer bouquet.

Materials

- Deep yellow cardstock, A4 (letter) size and 150gsm or less (for the centre)
- Yellow paper, A4 (letter) size and 80gsm or less (for the centre)
- White plain printer or photocopy paper (for the petals)
- Paper-covered floristry wire, roughly 16 gauge
- Dark green floristry crepe tape
- Hot glue (or double-sided tape)

Tools

- Paper scissors
- Wire cutters
- Glue gun
- Ruler (optional)
- Pencil (optional)

NOTE: while this classic daisy comprises a warm yellow and white contrasting petals, feel free to experiment. Go wild using these techniques with whatever colours you feel like creating with!

1.
2.
3.
4.
5.
6.
7.
8.

9.

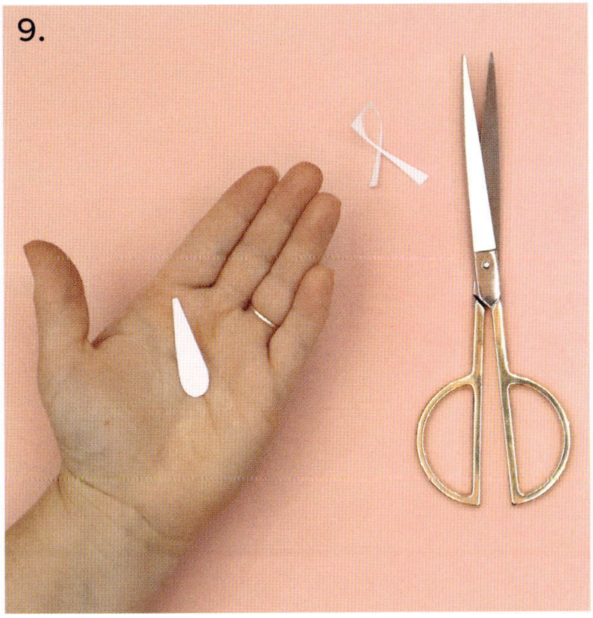

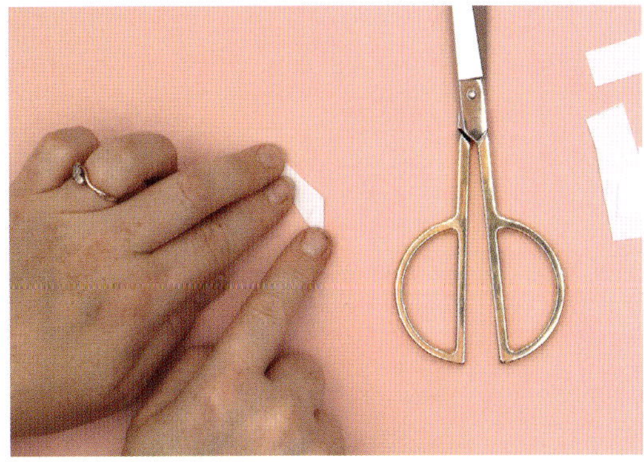

OPTIONAL STEP
Once you are happy with each petal, you could fold and crease each petal in half to create the ridges and folds in the natural oxeye daisy petals – however, the flower would still look lovely without this step!

1. Start by making the centre of the daisy. Measure and cut a rectangle 1½in (40mm) wide and 8¼in (210mm) long from the yellow cardstock using paper scissors.

2. Fold in half widthways so you have an 8¼in (210mm) long and ¾in (20mm) wide folded piece.

3. On the folded edge side, cut into the strip in 1/32in (1mm) or less increments to create a frilled-edge effect. Leave a minimum of a ¼in (5mm) edge at the bottom of the strip. Be careful not to cut all the way through, but don't worry if you do; you can simply join these pieces together as you assemble.

4. Take the floristry wire and cut to roughly 12in (300mm), if required. Starting at one of the shorter edges of the rectangle, using hot glue or double-sided tape, glue the wire into position about halfway (⅜in/10mm) into the rectangular strip. Ensure the folded, frilled edge is at the top.

5. Wind the cardstock around the wire as tightly as possible, gluing to secure as you go. Try to keep the paper level to ensure you create one solid flat-topped centre piece.

6. Once glued into position, repeat steps 1–3 using the lighter-weight yellow paper to mimic a daisy's natural change of texture. If you have only one type of cardstock or paper, you can still make the daisy in the same way – just continue using whatever paper it is you have. The techniques will still work; these are just guidelines as to what I feel would work best!

7. Now glue the frilled paper around the cardstock piece as before.

8. Next, cut rectangles for the daisy petals using the white printer/photocopy paper. Take the white photocopy paper and cut small ⅜in (10mm) wide and 1⅝in (40mm) long rectangles for as many petals as you wish to add (I made 20 petals). If making a bunch of daisies, vary the amount of petals in each flower to create a balanced variety among them all.

9. Ideally, each petal should be roughly 1½in (40mm) in length and only roughly ⅛in (2–3mm) at the bottom, increasing to ⅜in (10mm) where it curves at the top. Take one of the small rectangles and start at the bottom, on one of the shorter edges just outside the middle point. Cut at a slight angle towards the top, curve around the top and go back down towards the bottom following a similar opposite angle. This will be a lot easier than it sounds! Some petals are naturally more curved, and some are pointier than others, so do not worry about them being exactly the same. Some petals even have small notches at the very tip, so you could always add this too if you wanted a more 'random' natural finish.

10.

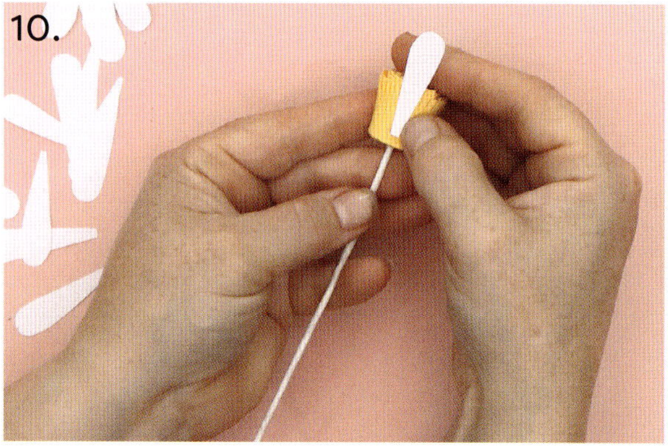

11.

12.

13.

14.

15.

IDEA!
Rather than using yellow cardstock and paper for the centre of this oxeye daisy, why not experiment by swapping them for a woollen felt ball. These are tactile and can often be found in colours matching a deep yellow oxeye daisy centre. Add the white petals and floristry crepe tape in the same way as detailed above.

10. Using either the hot glue gun or tape, stick the petals around the side of the centre point, slightly overlapping them. Oxeye daisy petals often have small gaps between each one, so they don't need to be at exactly the same spacing, as long as the petals go all the way around the yellow centre point. If some petals are slightly longer or shorter, you can balance them out at this point. Try to glue them so the top curved edges are at a similar level. Don't worry about any glue showing – it will all be hidden in the next step.

11. Once all of the petals are glued in place, grasp the flower around the centre, gently squeeze everything together, then lightly fold the petals outwards. You may find that there are some bigger gaps than you thought. If so, add additional petals to balance anywhere you feel they are needed.

12. Ensure you are happy with the petal layout before moving on to the next step of securing everything together and completing the stem.

13. Starting at the daisy flower end, attach the floristry crepe tape approximately halfway up the daisy blossom, ensuring all the petal ends are secured underneath the tape. Wind the tape around the flower before going slightly down towards the stem with one continuous piece of tape. There is no right or wrong angle to do this, as long as the daisy feels secure and you are covering all of the wire in greenery. If you want to, you could even do two or three layers of the tape for a fully green, opaque finish.

14. Once complete, slightly bend the daisy head so the wire is slightly curved at the top. This will help to display your daisy to full effect in a vase, bouquet or however you plan to use your bloom!

15. You are now finished! A simple, but beautiful oxeye daisy.

ADAPT!

You can adapt these techniques very easily for the small, grass level, simple common lawn daisy. This can be much fiddlier to make, purely due to the size, but it looks very pretty in a buttonhole, or just one in a very small bud vase.

- Starting with a ¾in (20mm) wide and 4in (100mm) long and piece of yellow cardstock, fold it in half into a ⅜in (10mm) wide and 4in (100mm) long rectangle.
- Cut into the folded edge in 1⁄32in (1mm) or less increments about halfway down the depth to roughly ¼in (5mm).
- Use a much thinner wire than the larger daisy for the stem – approximately 20 gauge wire. Use the same techniques to assemble as above.
- For the petals, use the frilling method. Cut a ¾in (20mm) wide and 4in (100mm) long strip of the plain photocopy/printer paper, and cut into it also with 1⁄32in (1mm) or less increments. You don't need to fold it. Each cut should be about halfway down the rectangle to a depth of roughly ⅜in (10mm).
- Glue on around the yellow cardstock, winding it as tight as possible.
- Try to keep the bottom of your white frilled paper at the same level as the yellow for an even finish.
- Once done, add floristry crepe tape to secure everything together, and open out the petals!

If you find the hot glue too fiddly with the small size of the flower, use double-sided tape.

Unlike the larger oxeye daisy, each petal will have a more squared top. As long as you keep the incremental frilled cuts as small as possible, this small flower can look very effective.

Persian Buttercup

Ranunculus asiaticus

These beautifully delicate flowers, more commonly known as ranunculus, may look complex at first glance, but fear not – they are much simpler to make than they may appear! While each flower does have lots of petals, they are relatively easy to assemble when you know how. There is such a wide variety of colours naturally occurring in these flowers, you really can get creative, and I can promise you that the final result will be worth it!

Materials

- Floristry crepe paper – a few coordinating tones, or opt for ombre paper (for the petals)
- Yellow or green ⅜–¾in (10–20mm) woollen felt ball
- Paper-covered floristry wire, roughly 16 gauge
- Green floristry crepe tape
- Hot glue

Tools

- Paper scissors
- Tapestry needle or sharp embroidery scissors
- Wire cutters
- Hot glue gun

FACT: the name 'ranunculus' translates from Latin as 'little frog'!

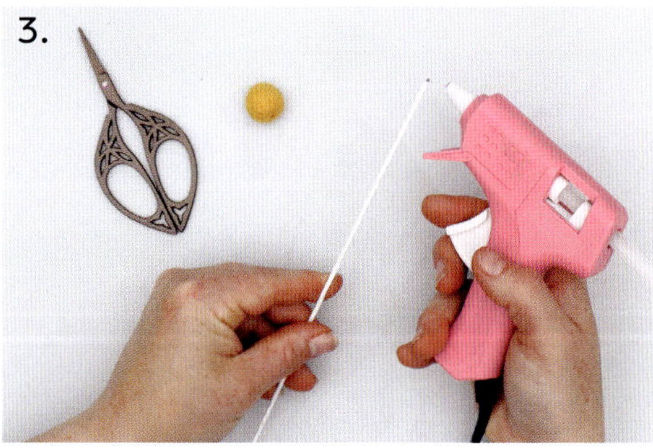

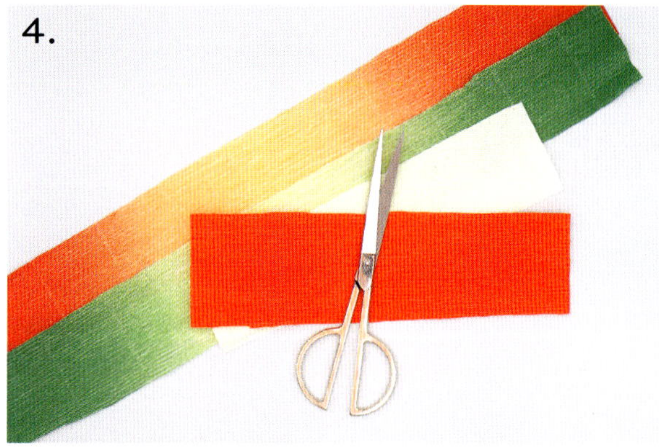

TIP
You can fold floristry crepe to cut more than one layer at a time. I often fold up and cut up to four layers at once. This really helps speed up the process; you will be amazed at how quickly 90 or more petals can be completed!

1. Start by attaching a woollen felt ball to the paper-covered floristry wire. It will become the centre point of the ranunculus flower head. Using the wire cutters, cut the floristry wire to 9¾–12in (250–300mm). If making a full ranunculus bouquet, try to vary the height of each flower so there is enough room to see them all.

2. Using the sharp tip of a tapestry sewing needle or embroidery scissors, very gently and carefully insert a small hole into the woollen felt ball – it will create a space to add the wire for a stem. You don't need to go all the way through – just roughly halfway to allow the wire to go inside.

3. Add a small amount of glue to the tip of the wire, then insert it into the new opening in the felt ball, attaching it securely. If you do not have a felt ball, you could use a polystyrene shape, wooden bead or even a dense pompom. You just need to start with a sphere before building the petals around it.

4. Most ranunculus petals are either all one colour or fade from dark to light (and vice versa). They often have a small gap of petals at the very centre, so you will need to replicate this as you assemble. You will be cutting 90 petals for this flower, so decide how you want the flower to appear colour-wise and cut the floristry crepe colours accordingly. I find it easier to cut strips of the colours used to make the paper easier to work with.

5. Start by cutting tiny petals ⅜–9⁄16in (10–15mm) long and 3⁄16–⅜in (7.5–10mm) wide that gradually increase to 1⅜–1⅝in (35–40mm) long and 1–1⅛in (25–30mm) wide. As long as the petals are approximately oval and you cut lots of them, you can stretch and layer to create the finished effect – so try not to worry too much about exact measurements. If you are making all of them one colour, this will make things much more simple, but it is certainly fun to experiment with different colours all together in the one flower! I find it easiest to start cutting the smallest, working up to the largest, but feel free to do whatever works best for you. I also find it easier to put together in groups of five or ten so I can easily see how many petals are already cut.

   As a guide, in this example I have cut:
   Smallest
   Darker green (ombre) 15
   Light green (ombre) 12
   Vibrant yellow (ombre) 10
   Pale yellow 17
   Peach (ombre) 8
   Coral (ombre) 20
   Largest
   Orange 8

If you cut some that are too big, you can just trim them down, and if you cut some that are too small, you can still add them in – you just might need to make a few extra. Sometimes I cut too many petals for what looks 'right' when making. I just save any spares for next time.

6. Once you have cut out the petals, create a curved effect by using your thumbs to push into the centre of each one. This will help to mould them around the felt ball and create that full flower form.

7. Now you can start adding petals to the woollen felt ball. Starting with the smallest petals, you will need to hot glue gun each petal in place. Start fairly high/central on the felt ball – don't worry if the bottom of the felt ball near the stem can be seen at this stage – all will be concealed much later. It can feel like a lot of glue, but with so many petals you will need to make sure they are extra secure.

TIP
Allow a small gap so the felt ball can still be seen in the top, centre part of the flower. Start working your way around it with the petals, overlapping each one. You will be amazed at how quickly it comes together!

8.

TIP
Some of the ombre papers have a much paler appearance underneath than the solid colours. Add the pale side face-down so that the richer colour can be seen from the front of the flower.

9.

10.

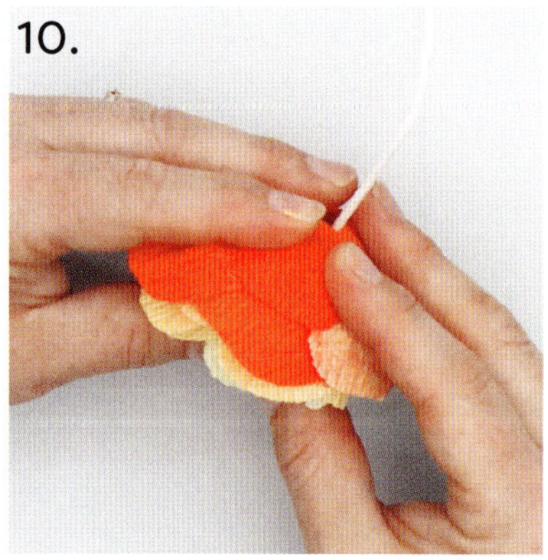

11.

12.

13.

14.

15.

16.

17.

8. Keep gluing at roughly the halfway up point of the felt ball, keeping the petals at roughly the same level until you have added half the petals. Now start working your way down. Attach the glue much further towards the stem, concealing the felt ball. This will help to make it appear like the flower is opening up.

9. Keep going until all of the petals are attached.

10. Once complete, squeeze the flower around the felt ball. This will help to bring all of the glue and paper together. Don't be afraid to also gently pull apart some of the petals to reveal some more than others – floristry crepe paper is pretty robust!

11. Now create a sepal for the base of the flower. On some of the larger ranunculus flowers, this may not be seen from the front, but it often can be when sitting in a vase, and it is particularly useful for smaller buds and flowers where the greenery forms part of what is visible. It also conceals all the petal ends at the base. Select a green floristry crepe paper and gently stretch it apart so it is completely without the creases. This creates a solid, flat piece of paper.

12. Cut a square roughly three-quarters the size of the flower head. Next, you want to create a 'thin leaf'-style pointed shape for every middle and corner of the square to create eight points in total, leaving a central space so they are still all attached – reminiscent of a Union Jack flag! I find this easiest to do by folding the square in half and then cutting to make everything symmetrical.

13. Unfold the sepal once the cutting is complete, then trim any points to make each one a similar length. I often find the diagonal points are longer and need adjusting.

14. Add a little snip about ⅛in (2–3mm) into the middle of the sepal – this is where you will push the wire through.

15. Add a small amount of glue to the underside of the flower before pushing the wire through the snip and the sepal up to the glue. If any of the cut points are particularly flopping down, add some extra glue to secure them in place.

16. Now add the floristry crepe tape. Starting just underneath the sepal – under the flower and at the top of the stem – start attaching it and work your way down the stem until it is completely covered with one continuous piece of tape.

17. When you look at a real ranunculus flower, the stems are often quite flexible; they bend in unexpected places and have curves and turns, particularly the smaller buds. Experiment moving the stem wire around to make waves until you are satsified with them.

BUDS

Buds need hardly any petals at all! Use exactly the same methods but use only 10–15 petals around the felt ball, then mould the sepal much further up and around the assembled piece.

SMALLER VERSIONS

Follow the same methods as above, but experiment using a lot fewer petals. Obviously, all ranunculus have the same amount of petals, but they are just concealed among those buds awaiting to bloom. However, with the wrinkled and crinkled appearance of floristry crepe, you can get away with much less. Some in the example shots contain just 30–50 petals!

Daffodil

Narcissus

A beautiful bunch of daffodils is something that often adorns my home as soon as the seasons allow. This iconically spring bloom is a special flower to me as 'Daffodil' is my nickname from my lovely mother-in-law, Heather. These cheerful paper varieties will allow you to enjoy spring all-year-round. The smaller dwarf tête-à-tête variety is a perfect make for buttonholes.

Materials

- Floristry crepe paper, yellows, or white/cream and orange (for the centre and petals)
- Paper-covered floristry wire, roughly 16 gauge
- 3 flower pips, yellow, double-sided
- Green floristry crepe tape
- Hot glue or double-sided tape

Tools

- Paper scissors
- Wire cutters
- Glue gun (optional)
- Ruler (optional)
- Pencil (optional)

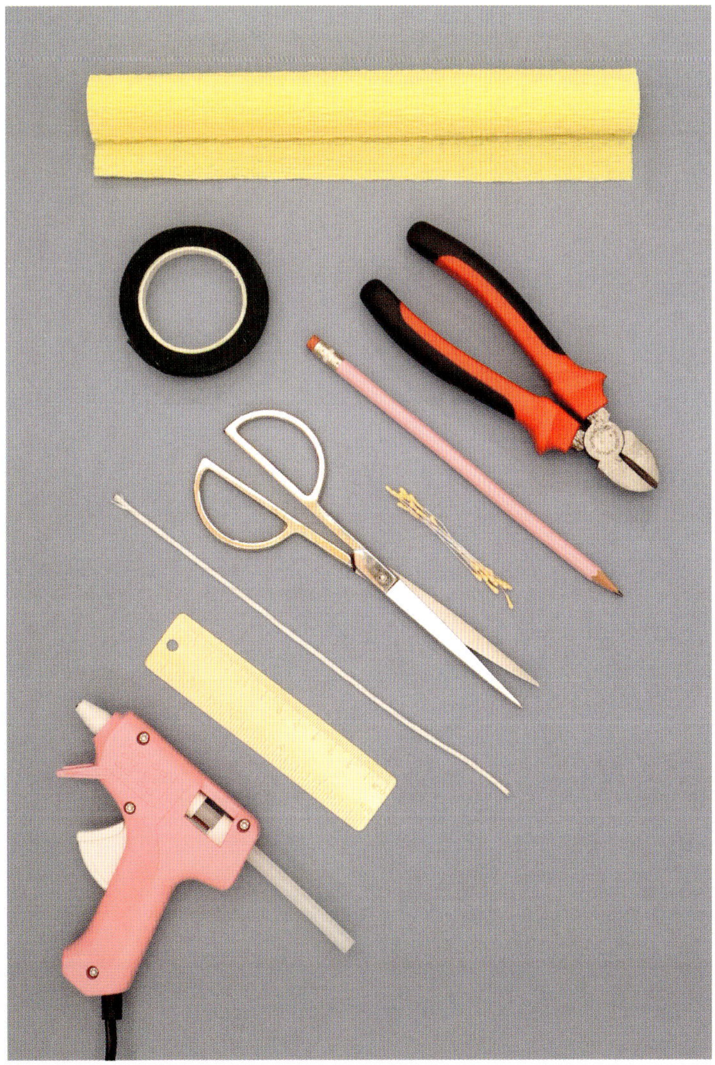

1.

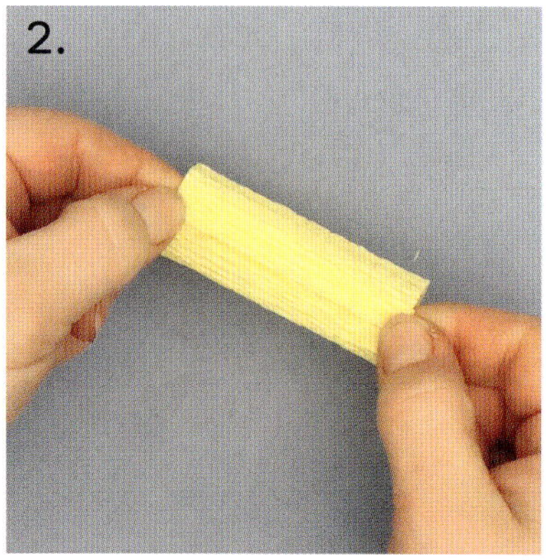
2.

3.

4.

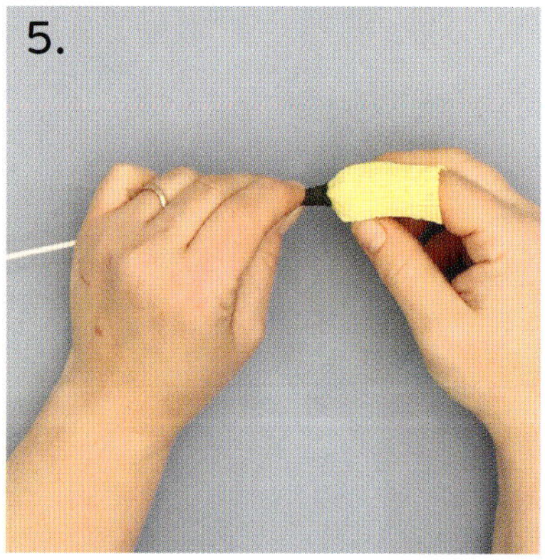
5.

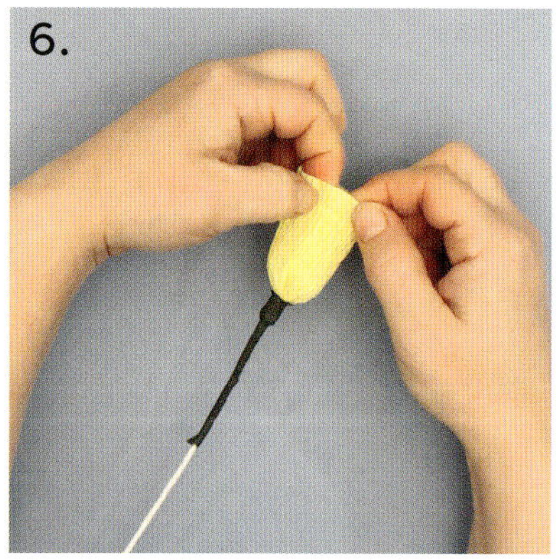
6.

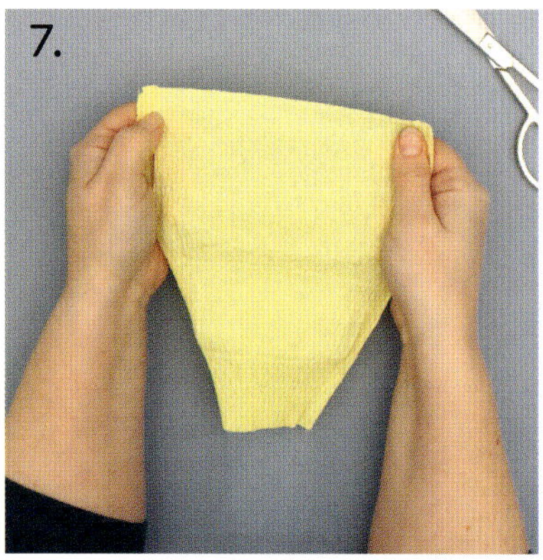
7.

8.

9.

10.

11.

12.

1. Start by cutting out the trumpet of the daffodil. Select the colour of crepe paper, then measure and cut a rectangle roughly 2¾–3⅛in (70–80mm) long and 2⅜in (60mm) wide. You will need the direction of the crepe grain to run along the width of the rectangle.

2. Fold into a tube shape. Slightly overlap the edges and fix into place using hot glue or double-sided tape.

3. Now take the flower pips and paper-covered wire to create the centre of the daffodil. Fold the three double-sided flower pips in half so you have six pips altogether. Slightly stagger them to create a natural look. Place on the tip of the stem wire, roughly ⅜in (10mm) from the end, before securing into position using the floristry crepe tape.

4. Place the trumpet tube (with the grain running up the tube) over the top of the stem wire and flower pips. Move the trumpet ⅜in (10mm) down from the tip of the stem wire, squeeze the tube inwards and secure into place using the floristry crepe tape.

5. With one hand, grip around the now secured trumpet and stem. With the other hand, gently push from the inside at the base of the trumpet outwards to mould a naturally bulbous shape.

6. At the top of the trumpet, pull the crepe gently apart periodically to create a frilled-edge effect.

7. Use yellow, white or cream floristry crepe paper for the petals. Stretch the floristry crepe paper completely out to remove all creases. This will create a smoother, more delicate and translucent effect to replicate the natural daffodil petals.

8. You will need six petals: roughly 1⅛in (30mm) wide and 2⅜–2¾in (60–70mm) long. You may find it easier to cut rectangles of this size before shaping them into petals, which will help keep the petals a similar size and shape. Some daffodils have shorter, wider petals, so experiment with these measurements if there is a specific variety you are trying to replicate. Cut them into a classic leaf shape, and leave a small narrow part at the bottom, which will help to attach them to the stem.

9. Add the petals to the stem wire, securing them just under the base of the trumpet. I find it useful to add three petals to each 'third' of a daffodil, before adding the remaining three in the gaps to complete the flower.

10. Once you are happy with the petal layout, wrap around the floristry crepe tape to secure everything together and complete the stem.

11. Bend the daffodil head so the wire is almost at a 90-degree angle to replicate a natural stem.

12. You are now finished! A beautiful spring daffodil.

ADAPT!

You can adapt these techniques to create the smaller dwarf tête-à-tête varieties of daffodil.

- Start with a 2–2⅜in (50–60mm) long and 1⅝in (40mm) wide piece of crepe paper for the trumpet.
- Make the petals 1⅝in (40mm) long and ¾in (20mm) wide.
- Use a 4–6in (100–150mm) long wire for the stem.
- Use only two flower pips.
- Use the same techniques to assemble as above.

Rose

Rosa

The beautiful rose has soft petals and a delicate fragrance. It is often associated with love, but did you know that every colour of rose has a different meaning? My lovely friend Hayley always buys me yellow roses, symbolizing 'friendship'. With so many natural colours and varieties of rose to get creative with, these floristry crepe versions are quick to assemble and so effective for a variety of purposes. These would look lovely in a big, blousy summer bouquet or among a winter wreath. I would love to see how you use yours!

Materials

- Floristry crepe paper (for the petals, any colour you like – even a variety of colours combined for a tonal or ombre look)
- Green floristry crepe paper (for the leaves)
- Paper-covered floristry wire, roughly 16 gauge
- Green floristry crepe tape
- Hot glue (optional)

Tools

- Paper scissors
- Wire cutters
- Glue gun (optional)
- Ruler (optional)
- Pencil (optional)

1.

2.
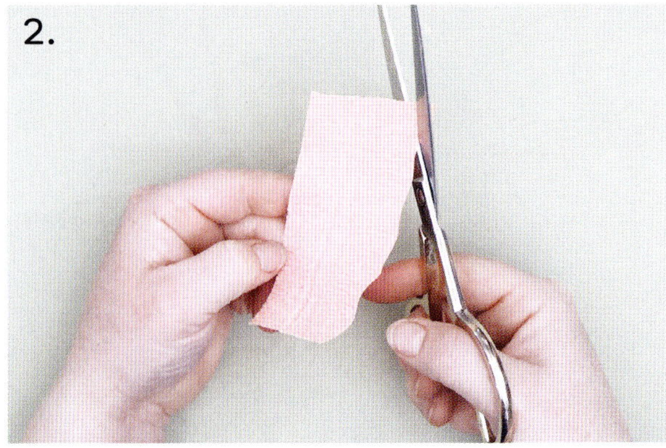

3.

4.
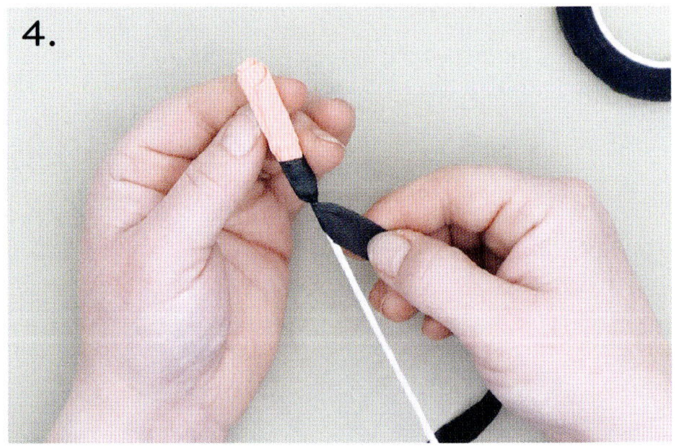

5.

6.

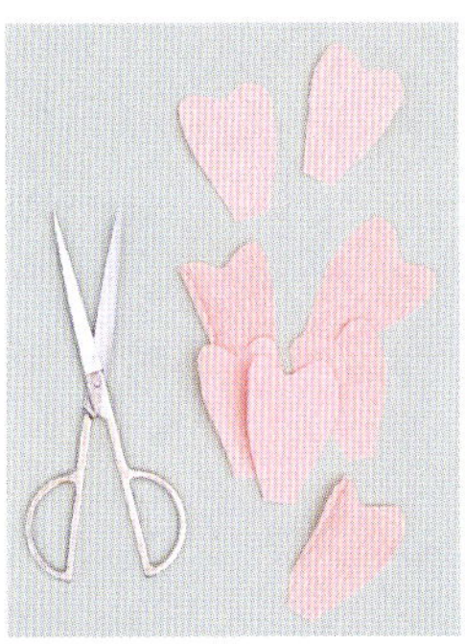

TIP
Experiment with the size and number of petals to create different effects. The larger the petals and heart shapes, the larger and more vintage style rose you will create. You can use fewer petals to make buds or smaller, enclosed roses.

7.

1. Start by making the centre of the rose. Measure and use the paper scissors to cut a rectangle 2–2⅜in (50–60mm) wide and 3⅓–4in (90–100mm) long from the floristry crepe paper. Keep the grain of the crepe paper going along the width of the paper to ensure this rectangle, and the shape of the petals, can be moulded.

2. Cut along the top of the rectangle to make a more wiggly edge. This will help to give a varied, more natural look to the centre of the rose.

3. Now position the floristry wire at one of the shorter edges of the rectangle, roughly halfway up, before rolling the paper around the wire.

4. Secure this rectangle into place using floristry crepe tape, or if preferred, you could apply glue with a glue gun.

5. To make the petals, you may find it easier to cut out rectangles before shaping the petals to keep them an even and approximate size. You will need six petals that are 2in (50mm) wide and 2⅜in (60mm) long, and eight petals that are 2⅜in (60mm) wide and 2¾in (70mm) long. Remember, you can layer the paper to cut more than one at once.

6. Cut the petals into heart shapes but make them with a longer, non-pointy base. You will use this base part later to attach the petals to the wire.

7. Using your thumbs, gently press down and stretch into the centre of each petal, moulding the crepe paper hearts into a curved petal shape.

8. You can also use a pencil to roll out the top edge of each petal, which will help to make the rose look like it is blossoming outwards.

9. Once all the petals are prepped into their new moulded shapes, you are ready to start attaching the petals to the stem. Starting with the smaller petals, attach each petal around the centre using a small piece of crepe tape for each petal. Try to keep the top of the petal 'level' with the centre piece.

10. Working your way around the stem wire, stagger each petal so they overlap. It may feel like a lot of tape is being used, but not only does it ensure that each petal is securely fastened to the rose, it also helps to create the naturally occurring shape of a rose.

11.

12.

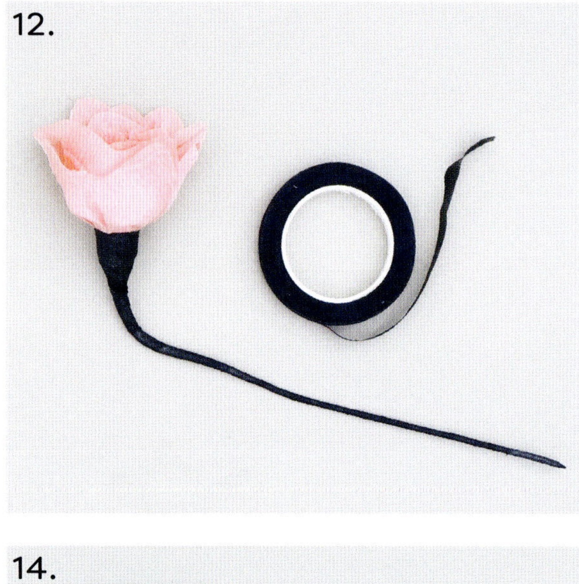

13.

14.

15.

16.

11. Once all of the petals are attached, you may feel there are gaps or that some petals need tweaking. You can always add an extra petal or two if you feel the rose needs it. You can also roll some of the petals further outwards using the pencil to do so. If you do this, grip around the central point at the base of the rose to ensure the petals don't get pulled out.

12. Once you are happy with the petals, wrap crepe tape around the wire to create the rose stem.

13. Take the green floristry paper and cut two leaves into a classic teardrop or leaf shape roughly 1⅝in (40mm) wide and 4in (100mm) long. These measurements include an elongated base, similar to the petals. It creates a section that can be attached to the wire stem.

14. Slightly snip into the very edges of the leaves roughly every ¼in (5mm) before slightly stretching apart to reveal a serrated edge.

15. Attach the leaves 2¾in (70mm) beneath the rose, using crepe tape on either side of the stem.

16. Slightly bend the rose head to create a more natural-looking angle, and you are done!

Sunflower

Helianthus annuus

Big, bold and bright! These summery flowers are full of sunshine. Sunflowers remind me of my lovely son Freddie. Not only are they joyful, but they naturally follow a mathematical sequence in their formation called the Fibonacci sequence, which Freddie knows by heart! These paper versions aim to replicate the multitude of patterns and texture of a sunflower's centre, surrounded by delicate and vibrantly yellow petals.

Materials

- Black thick cardstock, A4 (letter) size and 250gsm or more
- Brown floristry crepe paper (for the centre)
- Yellow floristry crepe paper (for the petals)
- Green floristry crepe paper (for the leaves)
- Paper-covered floristry wire, roughly 16 gauge
- Dark green floristry crepe tape
- Thin green floristry stub wire, roughly 22 gauge
- Hot glue

Tools

- Paper scissors
- Wire cutters
- Glue gun
- Ruler (optional)
- Pencil (optional)

1.

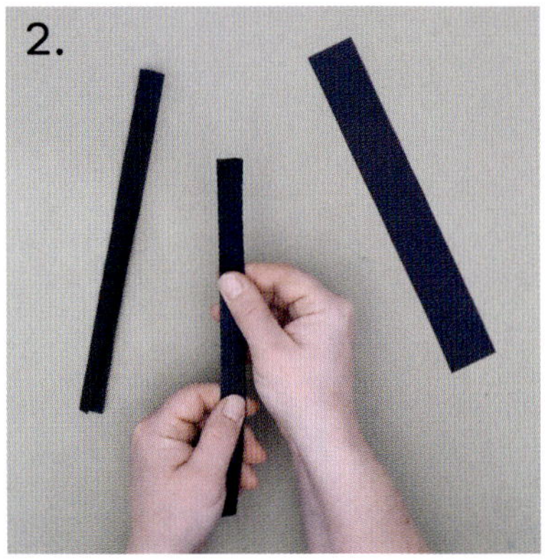
2.

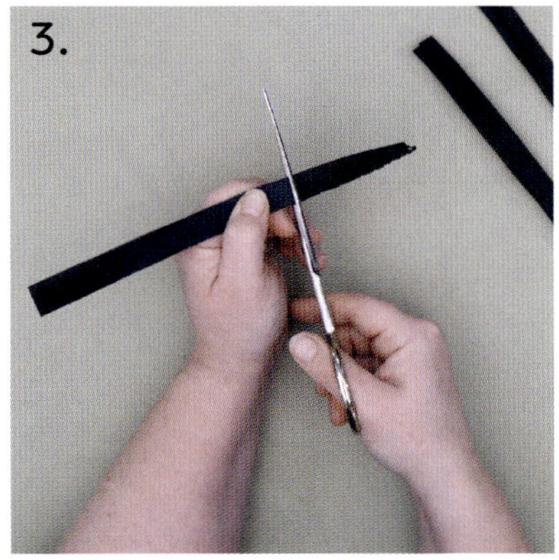
3.

4.

5.

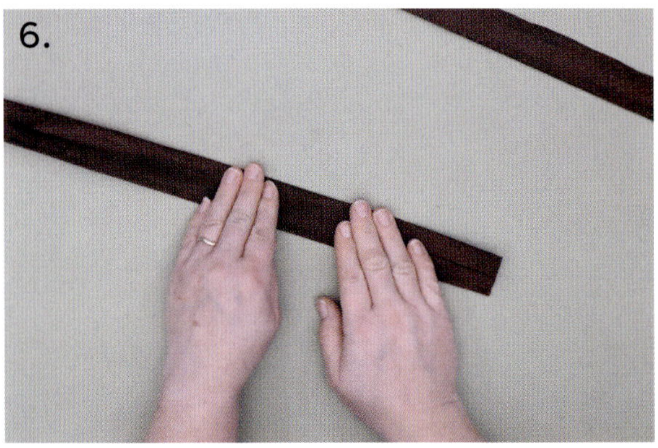
6.

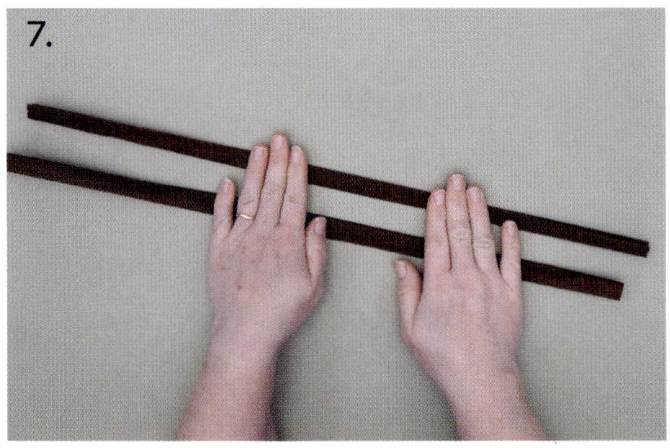
7.

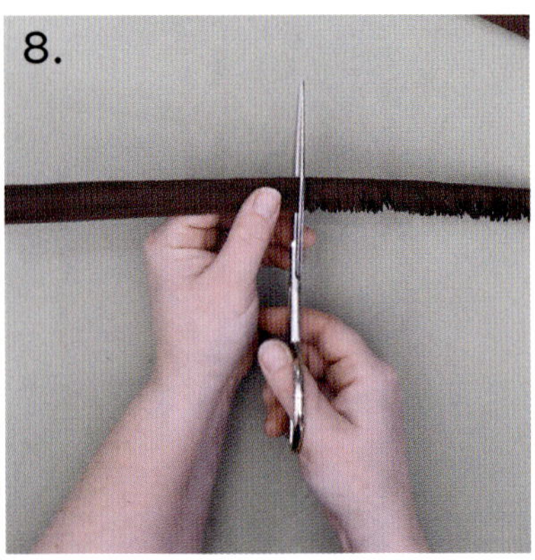
8.

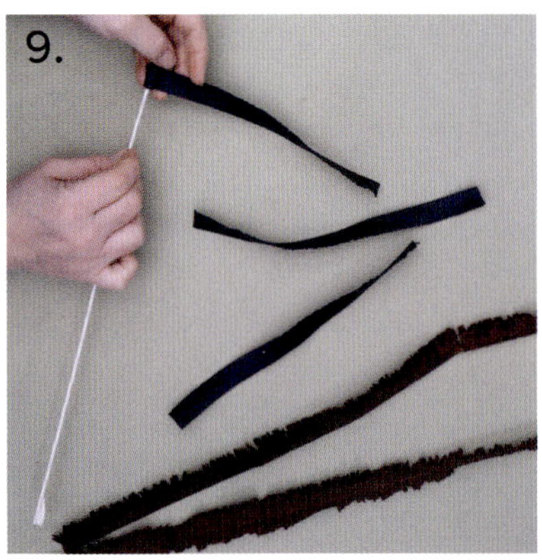
9.

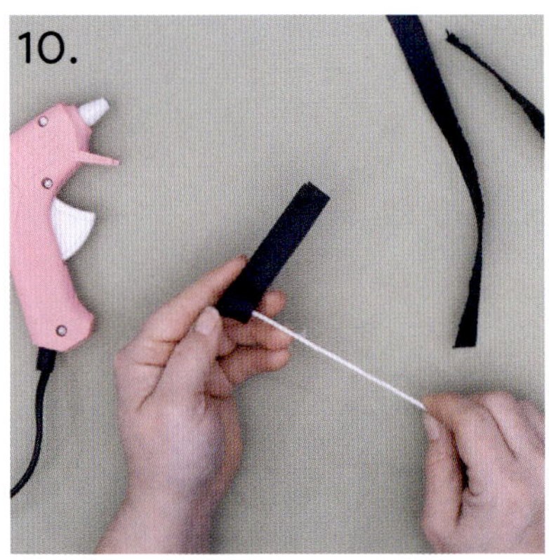
10.

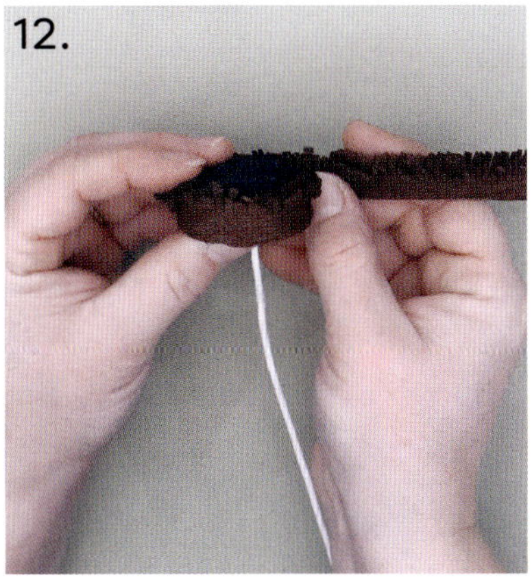

1. Measure and cut four rectangles 1⅛in (30mm) wide and 8–8½in (200–215mm) long from the black cardstock. If making a big sunflower, you can cut more rectangles of the same size to create a larger sunflower centre. Or if smaller – less! Experiment with the amount you use.

2. Fold each one in half widthways for 9/16in (15mm) wide and 8–8½in (200–215mm) long rectangles.

3. On the folded edge side, cut into the strips in roughly ⅛in (2–3mm) increments to create a frilled effect. Leave a narrow uncut band at the bottom of the strips to ensure everything stays connected.

4. Now cut two strips from the brown crepe paper 2⅜in (60mm) wide and 20in (500mm) long. It is important to ensure the grain of the crepe paper runs up the 20in (500mm) length of the strips to allow you to fold it easily in the next step. As with the black cardstock, you can have more or fewer strips depending on the sunflower size.

5. Fold a brown crepe paper strip in half to create a 1⅛in (30mm) wide and 20in (500mm) long strip, creasing it well.

6. Open the crepe paper out again, then fold each outside edge inwards, so they meet in the middle on the creased line, and glue into this position.

7. Now fold from the middle in half again, with the two folded edges together. You should now have a 9/16in (15mm) wide and 20in (500mm) long strip with four layers. Repeat steps 5–7 with the other rectangle.

8. Cut into this strip on the two folded edges side every ⅛in (3mm) or so to create a frilled effect.

9. Now take the stem wire and a black cardstock strip and, starting at one of the shorter ends of the rectangle, hot glue the wire into position roughly halfway into the cut rectangular strip. Ensure the folded, frilled edge is at the top.

10. Wind the cardstock around the wire as tightly as possible, gluing to secure as you go. Try to keep the paper at the same level to ensure you create one solid flat-topped centre piece.

11. Repeat with the remaining black strips.

12. Take the brown crepe paper strips and glue them on around the black cardstock centre in the same way. Don't worry too much if you end up with glue visible at the base – this will all get concealed later on.

13. If any brown crepe has stretched slightly while gluing on, trim back if required.

14.

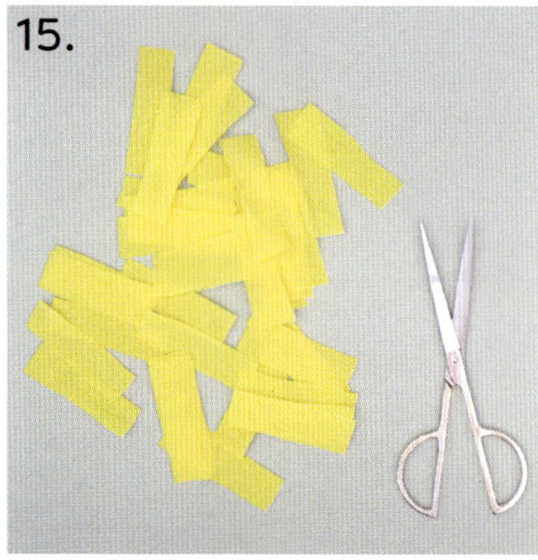
15.

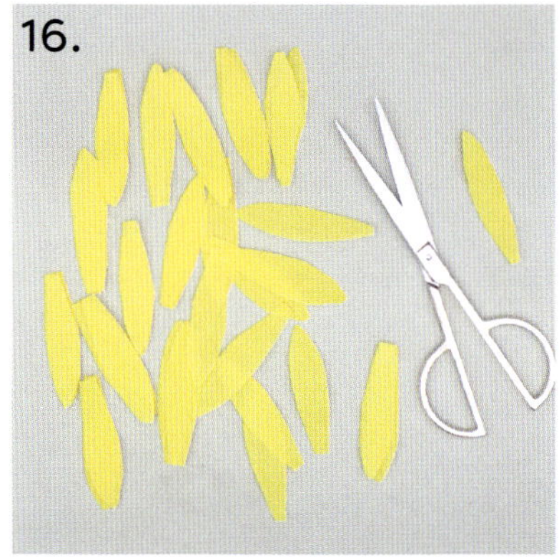
16.

17.

18.

19.

20.

21.

22.

23.

24.

14. To make the petals, stretch out the yellow crepe so it becomes smoother. This will help to create the naturally delicate sunflower petals.

15. You need to cut roughly 40 petals in total. Each petal is roughly ¾in (20mm) wide and 2¾–3⅛in (70–80mm) long. I find it easier to cut out rectangles of this size, before shaping them.

16. Cut out petals from the rectangles; they have a narrow bottom edge and tip with an elongated central section. Try to keep each petal a similar size and shape as sunflowers are naturally quite symmetrical in both construction and petal form. Some sunflower varieties have much shorter petals, and you can adapt accordingly if you prefer to create something different.

17. Starting underneath the sunflower, place one of the petal's base up close to the wire stem before gluing it into place below and up the side of the centre of the sunflower.

18. Moving incrementally around the flower, glue each petal into position. Overlap each petal slightly, trying to keep each overlap at around the same amount.

19. Keep going until you have completed one full round of petals. How much you overlap the petals will, of course, affect how many petals you need for this.

20. Make a second round of petals, placing each one in the gaps between the previous ones.

21. Now take the green floristry crepe paper, and cut eight elongated almond shapes. These will be used to conceal and form the base of the sunflower. The ones I have cut are roughly ⅜in (10mm) wide and 2⅜in (60mm) long.

22. Glue these to the base of the flower head with half on the flower, half down on to the wire stem. They should overlap slightly.

23. Keep going until all eight green pieces are attached.

24. Completely cover the stem wire with the crepe tape, wrapping it around to also conceal the ends of the greenery.

25. Sunflower leaves almost look like giant hearts! Cut out a heart from green floristry crepe. I find it easiest to first cut a rectangle 4in (100mm) long and 3⅛in (80mm) wide. Next, fold it in half and cut half a heart.

26. Slightly snip into the very edge of the leaf roughly every ¼in (5mm) before stretching it slightly apart to reveal a serrated edge.

27.

28.

29.

30.

31.

32.

27. Take the thin floristry stub wire and cut to roughly 4¾in (120mm), then place it in the middle of the leaf, roughly two-thirds of the way in.

28. Glue the wire into position and fold the heart up around the wire. This will create the very definite central crease of a sunflower leaf.

29. Open the leaf back out.

30. Bend the wire inside the leaf slightly to create that natural curved look.

31. Now use floristry crepe tape to attach the wire end to the main sunflower stem.

32. Repeat to make the other leaf. And you are finished! You could add further leaves, if desired.

Poppy

Papaver rhoeas

The poppy is iconically associated with remembrance, particularly in the classically vibrant red. However, poppies can also be found in a multitude of colours. Oranges, yellows, pinks and purples - even blue. Once cut, real poppies last only a very short space of time, but these paper versions can last forever!

Materials

- Red floristry crepe paper (for the petals)
- Black floristry crepe paper (for the centre and stamens)
- Any colour ⅜–⁹⁄₁₆in (10–15mm) woollen felt ball
- Paper-covered floristry wire, roughly 16 gauge
- Dark green floristry crepe tape
- Hot glue

Tools

- Paper scissors
- Wire cutters
- Fineliner or felt-tip pen
- Glue gun
- Ruler (optional)
- Pencil (optional)

1.

2.

3.

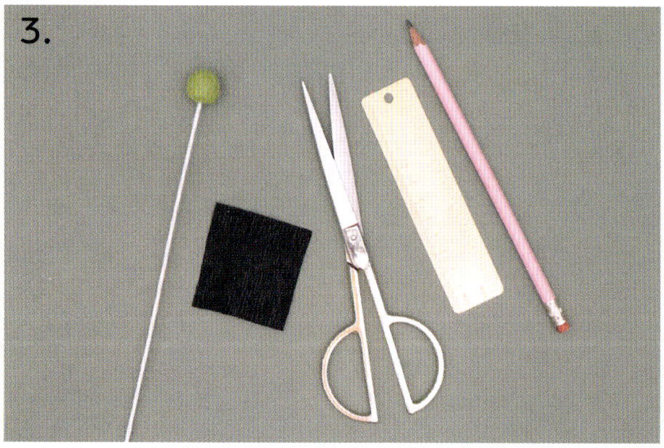

4.

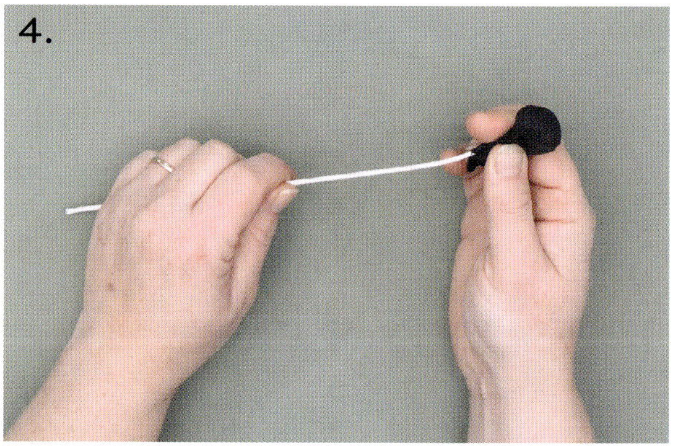

5.

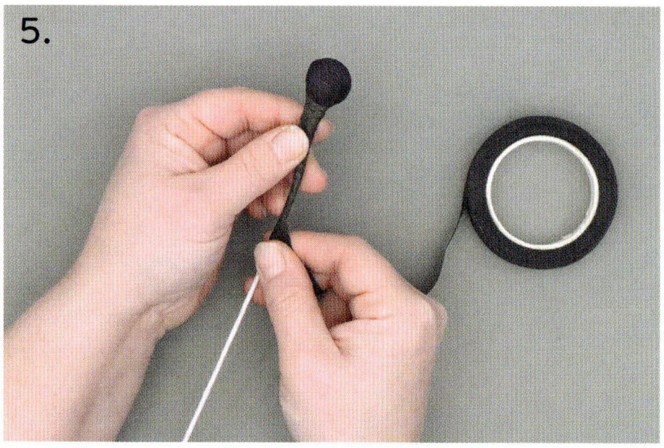

6.

7.

8.

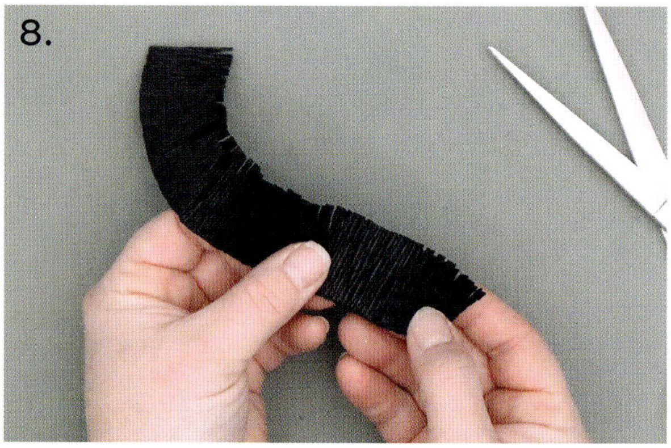

9.

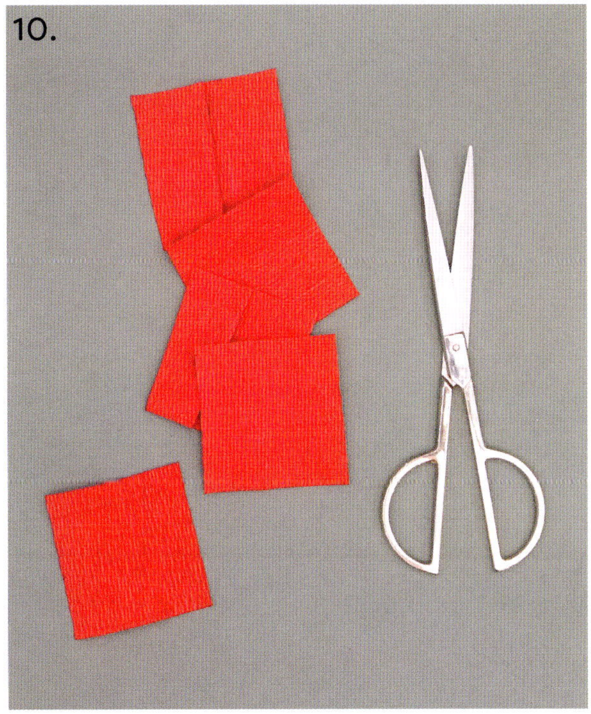

10.

1. To make the centre, using a tapestry sewing needle or sharp embroidery scissors, very gently and carefully insert a small hole into the woollen felt ball. This will create the space for the stem wire. You don't need to go all the way through, just roughly halfway to allow the wire to go inside.

2. Add a small amount of glue to the tip of the wire, then insert it into the new opening within the felt ball to attach it securely.

3. Cut a roughly 2in (50mm) square from the black crepe paper for the poppy centre.

4. Mould this square over the top of the woollen felt ball to create a smooth sphere.

5. If bulky, trim away any excess paper from underneath, but ensure there is still enough to have something to attach to the stem wire. Using floristry crepe tape, attach to the stem wire just under the felt ball.

6. Draw lines across the sphere with the fineliner pen. Make eight lines going outwards from the centre, each one at 45 degrees from the central point. Alternatively, you can draw these lines on the flat crepe paper before moulding it onto the woollen felt ball. I like to do it once it's moulded to ensure the lines are central. Even if you are using black crepe paper, I still draw the lines on. It's such a small touch but it helps to make the poppy look realistic. Or, consider using a paler paint-style pen so the lines are more vivid in appearance.

7. Cut a rectangle 2⅜in (60mm) wide and 6in (150mm) long for the stamens. If making a smaller poppy, this may need to be adjusted. You can trim to make it smaller widthways if you think this will suit the poppy better. Make sure the grain runs along the width.

8. Fold the rectangle in half widthways so it is now 1⅛in (30mm) wide and 6in (150mm) long. On the open edge side, cut into the strip in 1⁄32in (1mm) or less increments to create a frilled effect. Take care not to cut all the way through, making sure to leave an uncut band at the base.

9. Using hot glue, attach the frilled edge around the central point.

10. Next, create the poppy petals. Cut five rectangles 2⅜in (60mm) wide and 2¾in (70mm) long.

11.

12.

13.

14.

15.

16.

11. Now cut into each rectangle to shape them into wide teardrop-shaped petals, with the grain running up the petals. Allow for a small base, and keep them quite flat and wide, similar to a hot-air balloon shape.

12. Gently stretch the petals in the middle so they are slightly curved. Pleat them up and scrunch to create irregular ripples and ridges – poppy petals are quite crinkled looking! Floristry crepe paper is quite strong, so don't be afraid to really play with it. You could even screw up the petal before opening it out again – we don't want the petals to look perfect.

13. Once you are happy with the petals, start to add them to the centre piece. Add some glue underneath the flower base and at the very bottom of the sides to attach each petal.

14. Move around the poppy centre, adding each petal, one next to the other.

15. Now with all the petals attached, feel free to tweak them again. Pleat, fold, even stretch the petals again, if required, to make them appear uneven. Also feel free to bend and twist some of the frilled edges of the poppy centre slightly to make the flower look slightly less symmetrically perfect – the natural stamens do go off at different directions on a poppy!

16. Completely cover the stem wire, wrapping the crepe tape around it. You are now done! A beautiful poppy.

IDEAS

Instead of crepe paper for the stamens, you could use ready-made flower pips. At steps 7-8, instead of paper, fold the double-sided pips in half and attach in small groups around the edge of the central point.

Another idea is to use a felt-tip pen to colour in sections of the petals before attaching them - some poppy varieties have dark sections around their centres.

Gerbera

Gerbera jamesonii

Naturally available all-year-round in a myriad of colours, gerberas are such a joyful flower to both make and display. Similar in assembly to the oxeye daisy, the gerbera combines simple cardstock and floristry crepe materials to create strong petals and varied textures.

Materials

- Pale yellow or green cardstock, A4 (letter) size, 150gsm or less (for the centre and sepals)
- Orange paper, A4 (letter) size, 80gsm or less (or other colour of your choice, for the petals)
- Floristry crepe paper, in a colour coordinating with the petals
- Paper-covered floristry wire, roughly 16 gauge
- Hot glue
- Pale green floristry crepe tape

Tools

- Paper scissors
- Wire cutters
- Glue gun
- Ruler
- Pencil

NOTE: gerberas can have slightly 'green' centres, or sometimes they can be dark brown or cream. In some cases they are similar to the petal colours. Experiment with colour combinations!

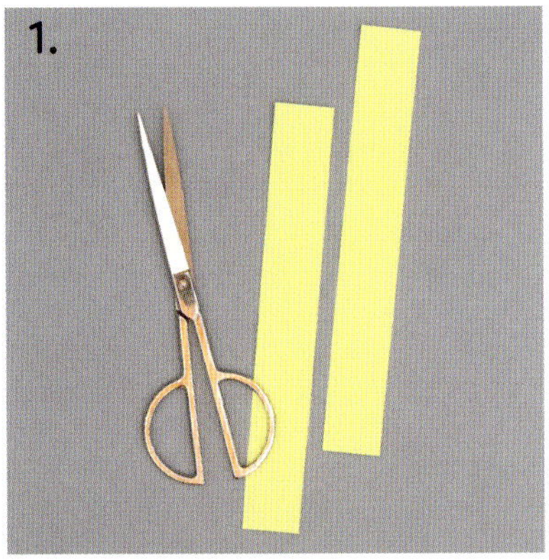
1.

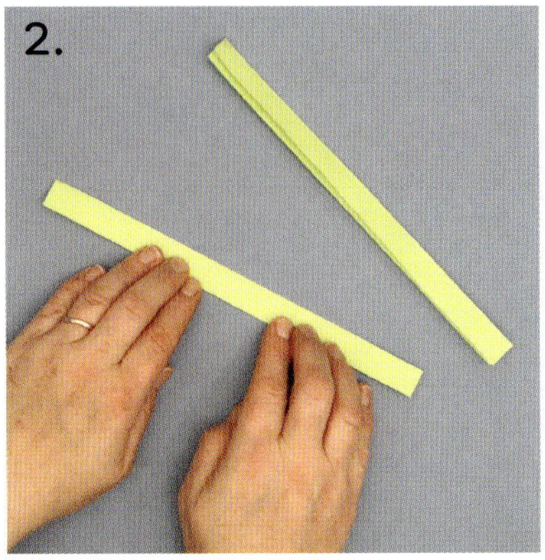
2.

3.

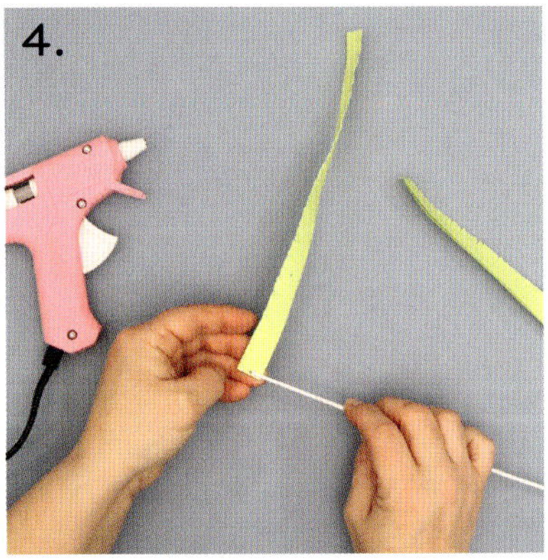
4.

5.

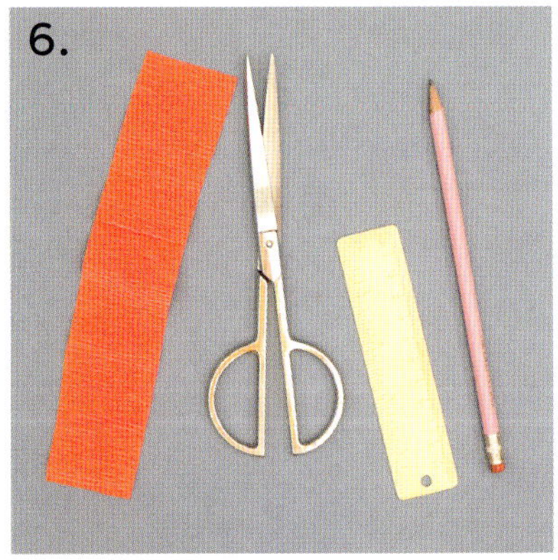
6.

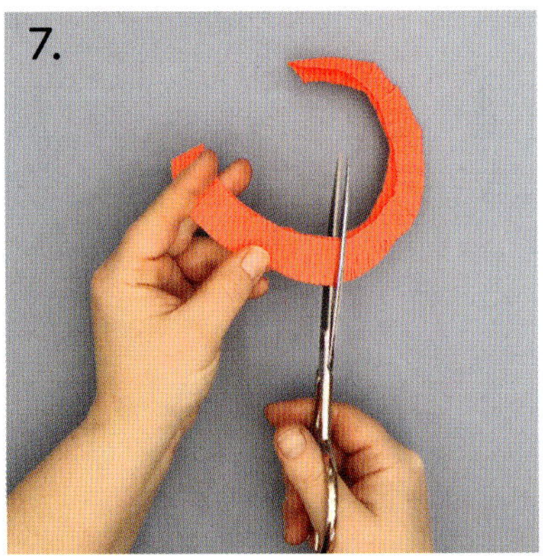
7.

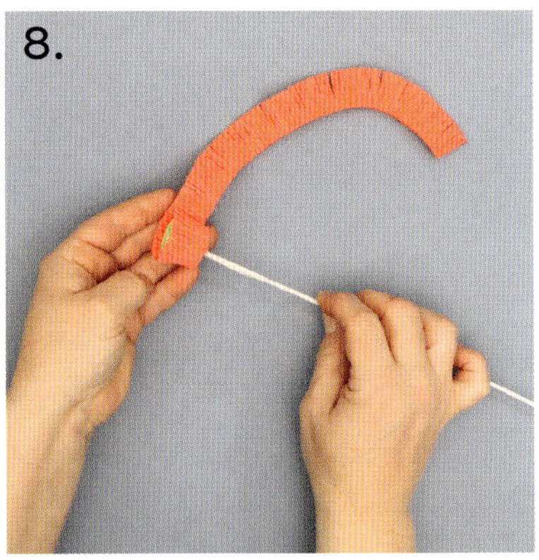
8.

9.

10.

11.

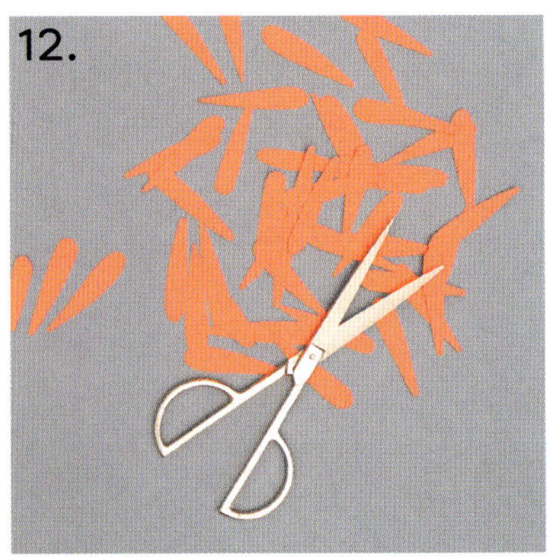
12.

1. For the centre, measure and cut strips from the cardstock that are roughly 1⅛in (30mm) wide and a total of roughly 16in (400mm) long. You can either use two strips of the cardstock or use cardstock scraps. There are many varieties and hybrids of gerberas, some with slightly smaller centres, so you can experiment with these measurements.

2. Fold the strips in half lengthways so they are now 9/16in (15mm) wide. Press down firmly to make sure the folded edge has a crisp fold.

3. On the folded edge side, cut into the strip in 1/32in (1mm) or less increments to create a frilled effect. Take care not to cut all the way through, making sure to leave an uncut band at the base. Do this for both rectangles.

4. Now take the floristry wire. Starting at one of the shorter ends of the rectangle, hot glue the wire into place halfway into the strip. Ensure the folded, frilled edge is at the top.

5. Wind the strip around the wire as tightly as possible, gluing to secure as you go. Try to keep the paper at the same level to ensure you create a solid flat-topped centre piece. Continue with the second rectangle.

6. Select your crepe paper and cut a strip 1½in (40mm) wide and 8in (200mm) long, with the grain running along the width.

7. Fold it in half so it is now ¾in (20mm) wide and 8in (200mm) long, then cut into the folded edge side in tiny increments to create a frilled effect (the same as on the original cardstock strips). Do not worry about keeping each cut exactly the same distance apart, but try to keep them as small as you can. They will help create texture around the centre point.

8. Now glue the frilled crepe paper around the centre.

9. Next, start to make the petals. You will need 50–60 petals in total. I find it easier to cut each petal from a rectangle to keep them a consistent shape and size. Cut three strips from the A4 (letter) size sheet 2⅜in (60mm) wide.

10. From these strips, cut ⅜in (10mm) wide rectangles so you have 50–60 small rectangles ⅜in (10mm) wide and 2⅜in (60mm) long.

11. To shape each petal, starting at the bottom of a rectangle, cut at a slight angle towards the top, make a curve and then go back down towards the bottom, following a similar opposite angle. Ideally, the petals will be only ⅛in (3mm) wide at the bottom, increasing to roughly ⅜in (10mm) near the top.

12. In addition to the 2⅜in (60mm) long petals, gerberas often have several slightly smaller petals, so cut a few that are only 1⅛–1½in (30–40mm) long. They will help to make the flowers appear natural and varied.

13. Once all the petals are cut, fold each petal in half to replicate the natural creases seen in a gerbera daisy. Fold them in half lengthwise before opening back out, leaving a crease in the card.

14. Starting with a few of the smaller petals, stagger them around the centre of the gerbera using hot glue to attach them.

15.

16.

17.

18.

19.

20.

15. Follow on with the larger petals, adding them all around the centre. If some of the petals are different heights, try to line them up at the same level at the top.

16. Gently fold out the petals occasionally to see if there are any gaps. Keep going until all the petals have been used. Don't worry what the ends look like at the moment – they will all be covered in the following steps.

17. Once all of the petals are glued into position, grasp the flower around the centre point and gently squeeze everything together, then lightly fold all of the petals outwards. If there are any gaps, cut/add some additional petals to balance anywhere you feel are needed.

18. Now cut along the width of the pale yellow or green cardstock to make a 1⅝in (40mm) wide strip. Cut 15 elongated almond shapes from this strip, which will be the sepals used to conceal and form the base of the gerbera. The ones I have cut are roughly ⅜in (10mm) wide and 1⅝in (40mm) long. You may need slightly more or slightly fewer, depending how much you overlap them.

19. Glue these to the base of the flower head, slightly overlapping each one and halfway up onto the flower to conceal any visible glue, with the rest remaining underneath the base.

20. Cover the stem wire by wrapping the pale green floristry crepe tape around it to finish. A lovely gerbera!

Echinacea

Echinacea purpurea

Echinacea is also known as 'purple coneflower' due to its striking central shape. It is actually a herb used widely for various medical remedies. While these paper ones can't fix your cold, they are super fun to make! The central brown texture contrasts with the vivid, hot pink petals to make a lovely combination. It can bring summer to you all year round.

Materials

- Brown cardstock, A4 (letter) size, roughly 150gsm (for the centre)
- Bright pink cardstock, 150gsm or more (for the petals)
- Green cardstock, 150gsm or less (for the sepals)
- Paper-covered floristry wire, approximately 16 gauge
- Dark green floristry crepe tape
- Hot glue

Tools

- Paper scissors
- Wire cutters
- Glue gun
- Brown felt-tip pen (optional)
- Ruler
- Pencil

1.

2.

3.

4.

5.

6.
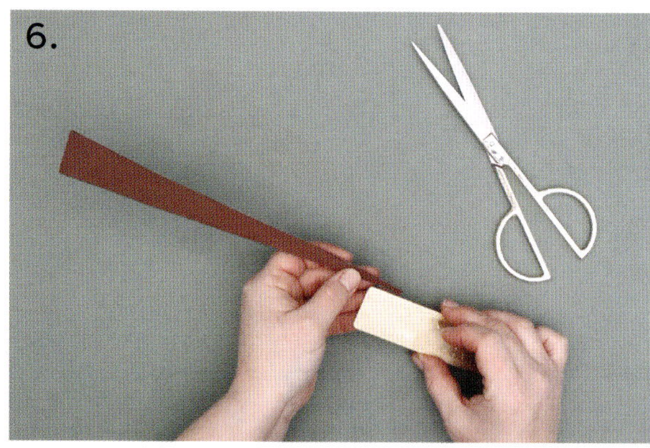

7.
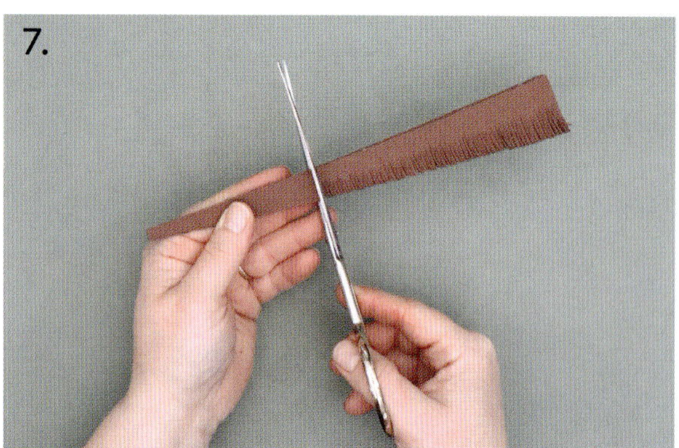

8.

1. To make the centre of the echinacea, measure and cut two 1⅛in (30mm) wide and 8¼in (210mm) long rectangles from the brown cardstock.

2. Using the ruler, draw a diagonal line across each rectangle from one corner to the other. If you haven't got a long enough ruler, use the edge of a sheet of cardstock to ensure a straight line. Cut along these lines to create four triangle shapes.

3. Turn the triangles so they all face the same direction; this will make them easier to glue in the next step. You want all the long, straight edges at the bottom, and the diagonal cut at the top.

4. Run hot glue along the bottom straight edge of each triangle.

5. Leaving the diagonal edge open and unglued, stick them all together so that each one is lined up, one on top of the other, until you have a four-layered triangle.

6. When they are all stuck together, cut off roughly ¾in (20mm) from the smallest end of the triangle.

7. On the diagonal side, cut into all four layers of the triangle in roughly 1⁄32in (1mm) increments to create a frilled-edge effect. This may be difficult at the smaller end of the triangle. Take care not to cut all the way through, leaving a small uncut band at the base. If you do cut through it, you can simply join these pieces together as you assemble the flower.

8. Now take the floristry wire. Starting at the longer edges of the triangle, glue the wire into place inside and roughly ⅜in (10mm) upwards.

9. Wind the card around the wire, gluing to secure it as you go. Try to keep the paper at the same level on the bottom edge to ensure you create a swirl down the centre piece with the diagonal edge. With the four layers together, it can be stiff to wind, but try to make it as tight as possible.

10. Once everything is glued into position, pull out and fluff the frilled edges to make the purple coneflower centre. Some cardstock has a white interior (rather than being a solid colour). If this is the case with the cardstock you are using, feel free to add some colour to the cut paper edges using a brown felt-tip pen.

11. To make the petals, cut 15–20 rectangles from the pink paper, making them ⅜in (10mm) wide and 2¾in (70mm) long.

12.

13.

14.

15.

16.

17.

18.

19.

20.

12. Cut out the petals. Starting with a narrow base, cut up towards the edge at the centre of one side before heading into a narrow point at the top and then back down the other side in a mirror image.

13. Once all the petals are cut, fold the length of each petal several times. This will create ridges and creases that mimic the natural texture of the flower and add character.

14. Glue the pink petals to the base of the centre piece, allowing for a small gap between each one. Try to glue them all at the same level so they are the same length.

15. Keep moving incrementally around the centre piece until all the petals are attached.

16. Cut a 1⅛in (30mm) strip from the green cardstock. From this 1⅛in (30mm) strip, cut 15–18 almond shapes roughly ⅜in (10mm) wide. These will be used to finish the base of the echinacea. How many you will need will depend on how much you decide to overlap each one.

17. Glue these almonds to the base underneath the flower to conceal any glue and secure everything into position, slightly overlapping each one.

18. Fold the petals out and downwards to mimic the natural form of a purple coneflower.

19. Wrap green crepe tape around the stem wire.

20. Bend the stem and you are finished!

Lily

Lilium

This elegant flower is often associated with peace. My grandmother was called Lilian and my niece is called Lilly, so I have always been drawn to these beautiful blooms. My mother is allergic to the pollen, so we could never have them in the house. However, these paper versions would be perfect! A few stems of these in a vase creates such a striking look, and they work well mixed into huge bouquets.

Materials

- Floristry crepe paper (your choice of colour, for the petals)
- Brown floristry crepe paper (for the stamens)
- Pale green floristry crepe paper (for the pistil)
- Dark green floristry crepe paper (for the leaves)
- Thin green floristry stub wire, roughly 22 gauge
- Paper-covered floristry wire, roughly 16 gauge
- Pale green floristry crepe tape
- Dark green floristry crepe tape
- Hot glue

Tools

- Brown felt-tip pen (optional)
- Paper scissors
- Wire cutters
- Glue gun
- Ruler & pencil (optional)

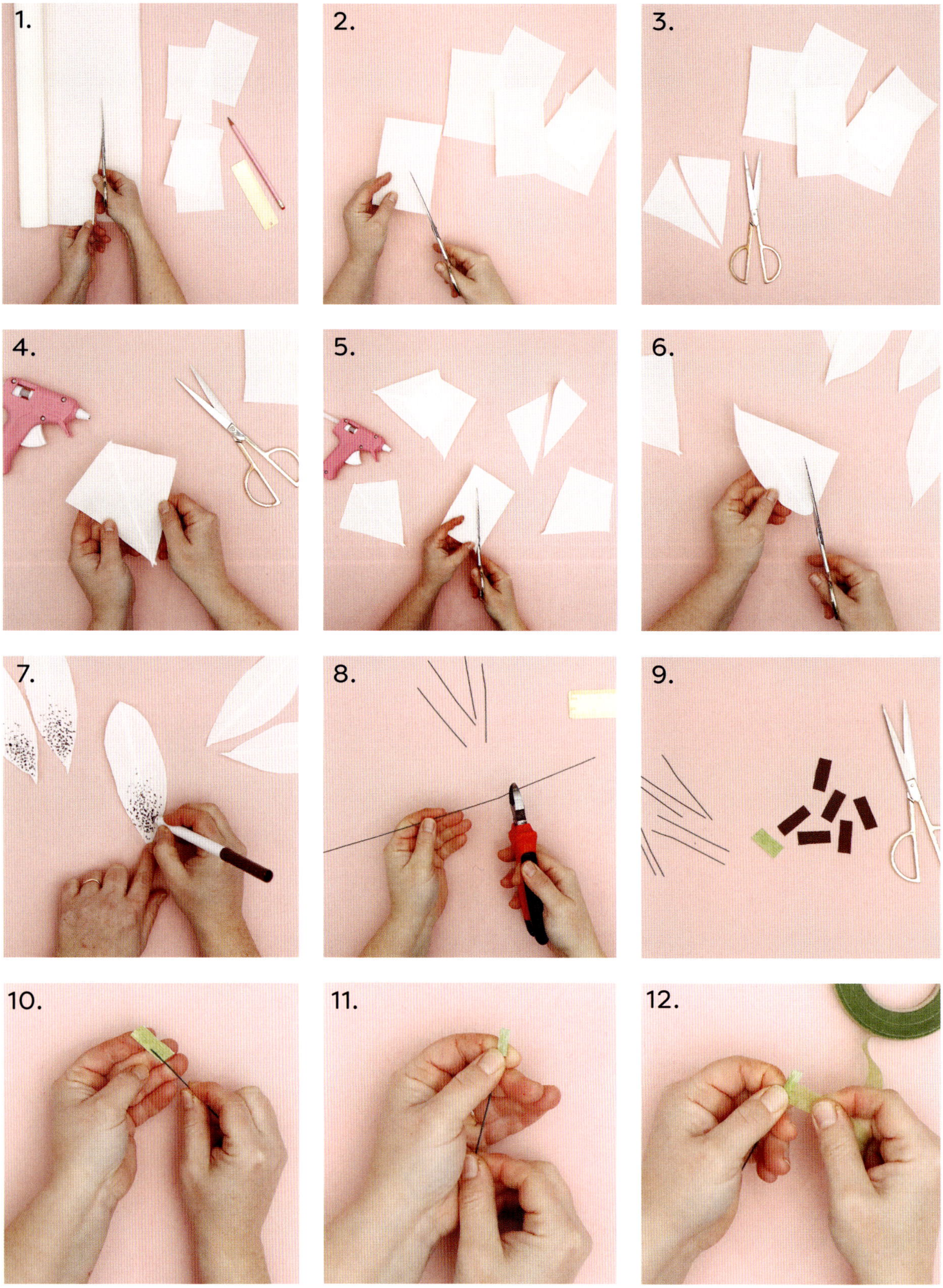
1.
2.
3.
4.
5.
6.
7.
8.
9.
10.
11.
12.

1. To make the petals, cut six rectangles 3⅛in (80mm) wide and 4¾in (120mm) long from the crepe paper.

2. Take one of these rectangles and cut diagonally across to make two triangles.

3. Turn one of the triangles over. You will see the grain will now meet in the middle. Ensure that the grain runs downwards into a 'V' shape towards you, not as an upside-down 'V'.

4. Run a small amount of hot glue along the diagonal edge of one of the triangles, then place the other triangle on top, just slightly overlapping them.

5. Repeat steps 3 and 4 with the other rectangles.

6. To shape a lily petal, keep the grain in the 'V' running downwards. Start off small at the bottom, curve up wide to the sides, then go back down into a smooth point at the top – much like an elongated, pointed oval. The finished petal will be roughly 2in (50mm) wide at its widest point and 5⅛in (130mm) long. Try to keep each side roughly symmetrical, using the overlapped part as the central point. Also remember to leave a wide-enough space at the base to attach to the stem wire later.

7. You could now add some little 'dots' on the petals – a bit like flower freckles! Use a brown felt-tip pen or similar and vary the amount of depth to the marks. Make some light and dark brown dots up to roughly one-third of the petal from the base upwards. You could experiment with adding colour to the floristry crepe – perhaps like the vibrant hot pinks of the Tiger Lily variety.

8. To make the central parts of the lily, cut seven lengths of stub wire, each 2¾in (70mm) long.

9. Cut one small rectangle of pale green crepe paper and six rectangles of brown crepe paper. Each one should be ⅜in (10mm) wide and 1⅛in (30mm) long. The grain of the crepe should run up the height of each rectangle.

10. Place one of the stub wire pieces halfway inside a pale green rectangle.

11. Roll the paper around the wire, then fold the top downwards so the wire is fully concealed inside.

12. Secure this paper into position on the wire using pale green floristry crepe tape, and completely cover the stub wire, leaving only the very tip of crepe paper exposed above the tape. This piece will go at the centre of the lily – it is the pistil.

13. Repeat with the remaining six stub wires and brown rectangles, but with a slight difference. When placing a stub wire inside the brown rectangle, place roughly one-third inside (instead of halfway as before). Roll the paper around the wire, and fold the top downwards so the wire is fully concealed inside before securing this paper into place on the wire with the pale green floristry crepe tape. There should be a small bit of the brown crepe above the wire top, which will be turned into the stamen in the following steps.

14. Squeeze the brown crepe paper together so it is quite condensed, then bend it at a slight angle to mimic the natural stamens of a lily.

15.

16.

17.

18.

19.

20.

21.

22.

23.

24.

25.

26.

15. Now take the main stem floristry wire and the green 'pistil' section. Attach the pistil to the stem wire with the dark green crepe tape, leaving 2in (50mm) of the pistil above the top of the stem wire. If you are making a large lily-only bouquet or a single stem lily, you may want to make the main stem wire 20–24in (500–600mm) in length to create a realistic lily height. Or, if you are planning to incorporate it with a mixed bouquet, you can, of course, use a much shorter stem.

16. Repeat with the brown stamens, attaching them slightly higher than the pistil. Try to make the stamen tops just above, but at an even height.

17. Slightly bend the stamens outwards.

18. To shape the petals before attaching them, using either a pencil or your fingers, bend each petal so it is curved in the middle. Roll under the very top of the lily petals so they curl underneath slightly.

19. Attach the petals around the central piece using the dark green crepe tape at the very bottom of each petal. Go down the stem slightly with the tape to ensure everything is secure.

20. Attach three of the petals into 'thirds' around the central point.

21. Follow on with the other three petals, placing them in the gaps.

22. Completely cover the stem by wrapping it with the dark green floristry crepe tape.

23. Push the petals gently outwards around the centre, then further shape the petals outwards, if required.

24. To add leaves, cut three or four elongated almond-type shapes from the dark green floristry crepe making them and roughly 1⅛in (30mm) wide and 5⅛–5½in (130–140mm) long.

25. Gently curve the leaves slightly.

26. Attach each leaf along the wire stem, ¾–1⅛in (20–30mm) apart going down the stem, using the dark green floristry crepe tape. Try to vary which direction the leaves go. And you are done – you have a lovely lily stem.

Peony

Paeonia

This is one of my favourite paper flowers to make. I absolutely adore peonies, with all those beautiful delicate ruffles. It has always been a dream to grow my own but, unfortunately, I cannot even get the plant to grow, let alone flower. I enjoy vases filled with handcrafted paper versions instead! This project works well either as a solo bloom in a single stem vase or with lots together to form a huge statement bouquet.

Materials

- Fine-weight floristry crepe paper (your choice of colour, for the petals)
- Peach or golden yellow floristry crepe paper (for centre)
- Green floristry crepe paper (for the sepals)
- Paper-covered floristry wire, roughly 16 gauge
- Dark green floristry crepe tape
- Hot glue

Tools

- Paper scissors
- Wire cutters
- Glue gun
- Ruler (optional)
- Pencil (optional)

NOTE: while you could use any weight of floristry crepe paper, the lighter 'fine' weight papers are a really good mimic of the delicate peony petals. Alternatively, you could use a heavier weight, but try to get the paper roll variety without the larger 'lines' running throughout.

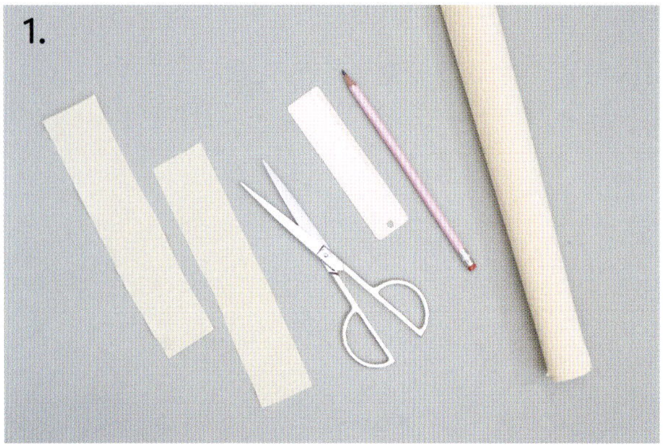
1.

2.

3.

4.

5.

6.

7.

8.

1. From the floristry crepe paper chosen for the centre, cut either two rectangles 1½in (40mm) wide and 8in (200mm) long, or just one rectangle 1½in (40mm) wide and 16in (400mm) long. Choose whatever works best for the paper you have.

2. Cut into the strip(s) at 5/64–⅛in (2–3mm) increments to create a frilled-edge effect. Take care not to cut all the way through, leaving an uncut band at the base.

3. Place the floristry stem wire at one end of the frilled rectangle(s), roughly ⅜in (10mm) from the edge, and glue it into position. The length of the stem wire will depend on how you wish to use the peony. Keep it 20–24in (50–60cm) long if you plan to use as a single stem or if you are making a peony-only bouquet. If you plan to nestle the peony into a larger mixed bouquet, you can use a smaller stem wire.

4. Wind the paper strip around the wire as tightly as possible, gluing to secure it as you go. Try to keep it level. Repeat with the second rectangle, if you have one, around the first.

5. Gently push the frills of this central piece slightly outwards so they are more varied and open.

6. For the petals, you will need to make various sizes in different amounts, so begin cutting the floristry crepe paper into rectangles in the dimensions below. Make sure the grain of the paper runs up the height of the petal.

   Small (14): 2⅜in (60mm) long and 1½in (40mm) wide
   Medium (12): 2¾in (70mm) long and 2in (50mm) wide
   Large (5): 3⅛in (80mm) long and 2⅜in (60mm) wide

   If you want to make the peony smaller, you can use fewer petals. To make a very large peony, add a further 5–8 large petals.

7. I think of peony petals as sort of heart shapes, but with a wider base. Mix them up so you have a variety of different top edges. Make some with one dip like a heart and some with two. The dips you cut into the top don't need to be centred – try to keep them varied. They will add character to the peony and add to the ruffled look.

8. Once you have shaped all of the petals, you need to mould them. Using your thumbs, gently press into the centre of each petal to slightly stretch the crepe and create a curved shape.

9. Starting with the smallest petals, glue the petals incrementally around the central point. Ensure you apply glue only at the bottom of each petal to allow the flower to be quite open.

10. Work your way around the centre, slightly overlapping each petal. Try to keep the top of the petals at a similar height.

11.

12.

13.

14.

15.

16.

17.

11. Move on to the medium petals and continue to attach them around the flower.

12. Once you start getting to the large petals, you might find it harder to keep the tops at the same height. Don't worry – as you keep adding the petals, they will naturally start opening outwards just like a blossoming peony!

13. Once all of the petals are added, the next stage is to create the sepals. Cut five rectangles from the green floristry crepe paper roughly 1⅛in (30mm) wide and 1½in (40mm) long.

14. Cut them into wide almond shapes.

15. Glue the sepals around the stem at the base of the peony so they are halfway on the flower and halfway down the stem wire.

16. Once the sepals have all been added, secure them in place with the green crepe tape. Completely wrap the tape around the stem to cover it.

17. You are now finished! A stunning petal-filled peony flower.

Anemone

Anemone coronaria

Anemones carry many varied meanings around the world. Some say they bring good luck, others that they are used as beds by fairies! This striking flower has dark and strong centres that contrast with its slight and delicate fluttering petals. This project utilizes a variety of techniques to replicate their natural textures. The flowers look lovely on their own or in a spring posy.

Materials

- Black or dark grey $^{9}/_{16}$in (15mm) woollen felt ball
- White or cream floristry crepe paper (for the centre)
- Floristry crepe paper (your choice of colour, for the petals)
- Green cardstock, A4 (letter) size and 150gsm (for the leaves)
- Paper-covered floristry wire, roughly 16 gauge
- Hot glue
- Green floristry crepe tape

Tools

- Paper scissors
- Wire cutters
- Glue gun
- Tapestry needle or sharp embroidery scissors
- Black or dark grey felt-tip pen
- Ruler
- Pencil

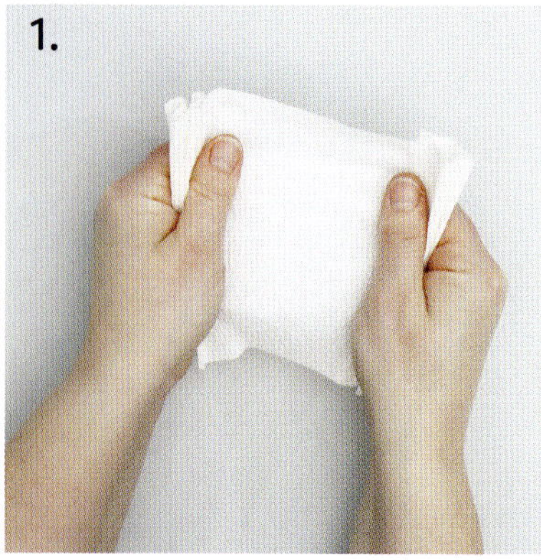
1.

2.

3.

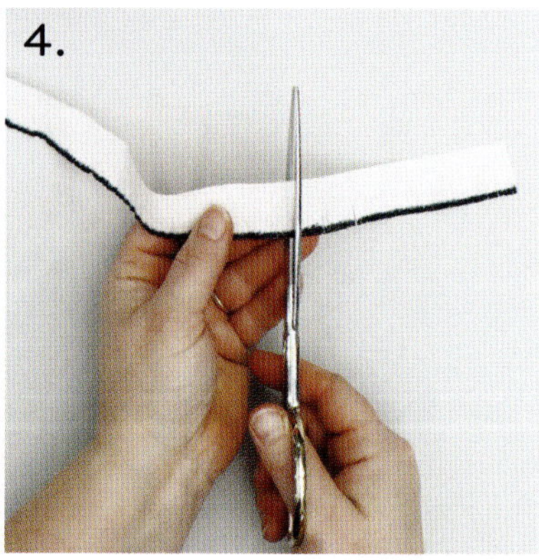
4.

5.

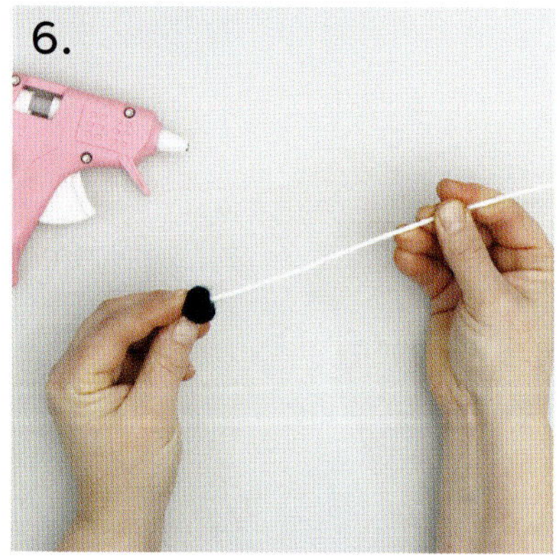
6.

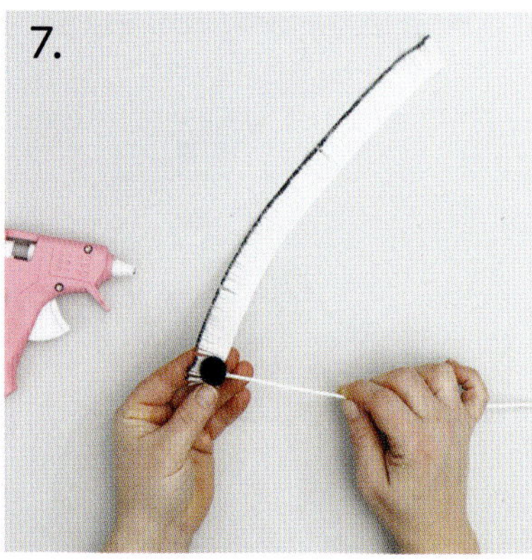
7.

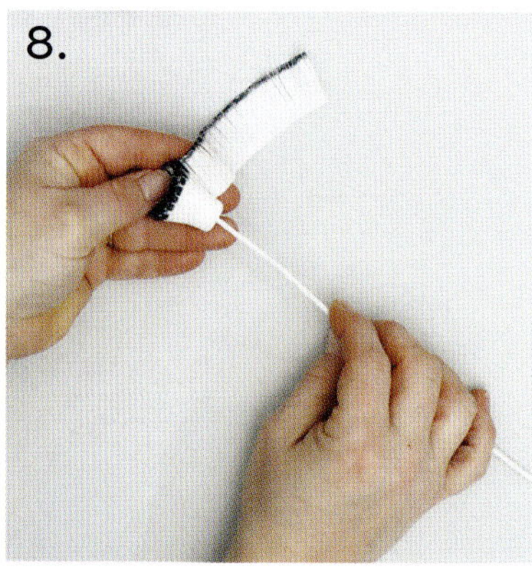
8.

9.

10.

11.

12.

13.

14.

1. Stretch out some of the white or cream crepe paper so it becomes much smoother. When stretched, you will only need a thin piece roughly ¾in (20mm) wide and 12in (300mm) long. This technique allows a small amount of the white to be visible, which provides a nice definition against the dark anemone centre. Alternatively, you can use black crepe paper.

2. Measure and cut a strip of the stretched crepe paper to ¾in (20mm) wide and 12in (300mm) long, with the grain running widthways.

3. Using a black or dark grey felt-tip pen, add a roughly ¼in (5mm) wide band of colour along one long side. Turn the paper over and add colour on the same end, ensuring the black ink fully saturates both sides of the paper. Allow the ink to dry.

4. Cut into the strip along the coloured edge of the strip in 5⁄64–⅛in (2–3mm) increments to create a frilled-edge effect. Leave an uncut band at the base of the strip so everything stays together.

5. Turn to the stem wire and felt ball. Using the sharp tip of a tapestry sewing needle or embroidery scissors, gently and carefully insert a small hole into the woollen felt ball until around halfway through. It will create a space to add the wire for the stem. You can cover the felt ball in black crepe paper, if desired, but I prefer the contrast in texture that the felt ball gives the anemone.

6. Add a small amount of glue to the tip of the wire, then insert it into the new opening within the felt ball to attach it securely.

7. Place the felt ball centre at a short end of the white frilled-edge strip with the coloured end at the top. Glue it in place, attaching the strip mainly to the ball's sides.

8. Make sure to try to keep the strip level, so that you can see both the black edges and some of the white underneath, and wrap it around the centre, adding glue as you go.

9. Now stretch out the floristry crepe paper chosen for the petals to make it smooth.

10. Anemone petals can be quite varied in both size and shape. Start by cutting 8–10 rectangles 1⅛–1½in (30–40mm) wide and 2in (50mm) long.

11. To shape these rectangles into petals, start cutting at the bottom to create a small base to attach the petals to the main central piece. Then cut in a curve towards the top corner, across the top and down the other side in a mirror image. You can add some small dips and wiggles along the top of the petal, too – try to keep them varied!

12. Once cut, don't be afraid to push or pull the petals around a little to create some texture in them. While the crepe has already been stretched out, it will still have some movement. Anemone petals can often appear slightly crinkled.

13. Use hot glue to attach the petals to the central piece. Follow the base of the white piece as a guide to keep the base of each of the petals level. Move around the flower, attaching the petals so they slightly overlap.

14. Once all the petals are attached, cut small almond shapes out of the green cardstock to cover the base, making them ⅜in (10mm) wide and 1½in (40mm) long.

15.

16.

17.

18.

19.

20.

21.

22.

15. Glue them to the base of the flower head so they are halfway on the flower and halfway on the wire stem, overlapping each one slightly.

16. Use the crepe tape to secure the base of those almond shapes before wrapping it around the stem wire to completely cover it.

17. To make the anemone foliage, start by cutting a 2¾in (70mm) square of green cardstock for each leaf – plan on two or three leaves per flower. (You could use green floristry crepe paper, but cardstock more accurately represents the sharp, smooth foliage. Cardstock holds the structure much more, while floristry crepe paper is too thin and often folds down easily.)

18. Now trim the squares into anemone leaf shapes. It is hard to describe the shape of this foliage – think of seaweed, a bare tree or a curvy, grass-style shape. Or, if you prefer, you could cut several thin curvy strips and attach them together. The main thing is to leave a small base to attach them to the flower.

19. Once you have cut out the leaves, gently curl the strappy ends using your fingers.

20. Glue the base of the leaves to the flower, just below the flower head.

21. Conceal and further secure the ends of the leaves by wrapping crepe tape around them and continue to wrap it around the stem wire to cover it.

22. Gently tease the petals open to reveal the centre. You are now finished! A lovely anemone.

Cosmos

Cosmos bipinnatus

Cosmos has so many varieties – pinks, oranges, brown, white – that ombre crepe paper would also be a good choice for this flower. We have 'Apricotta' in our garden, and I love to watch them filled with buzzy bees and butterflies. While fine-weight crepe tends to replicate the delicate nature of the petals, heavier-weight crepe paper replicates their natural ripples and ridges – so choose whatever paper you have or would like based more on the colours you would prefer.

Materials

- Deep yellow cardstock, 150gsm or less (for the centre)
- Dark brown or black cardstock (for the centre)
- Floristry crepe paper (your choice of colour, for the petals)
- Paper-covered floristry wire, roughly 16 gauge
- Dark green floristry crepe tape
- Hot glue

Tools

- Paper scissors
- Wire cutters
- Glue gun
- Ruler
- Pencil

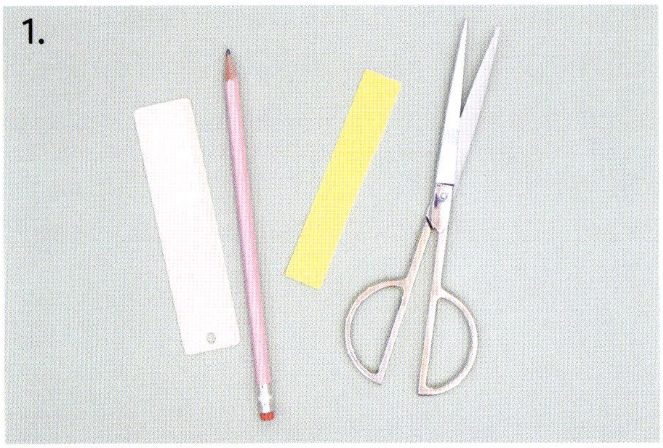
1.

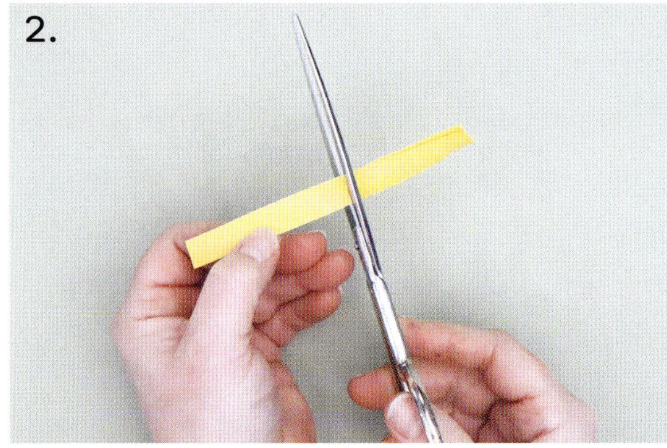
2.

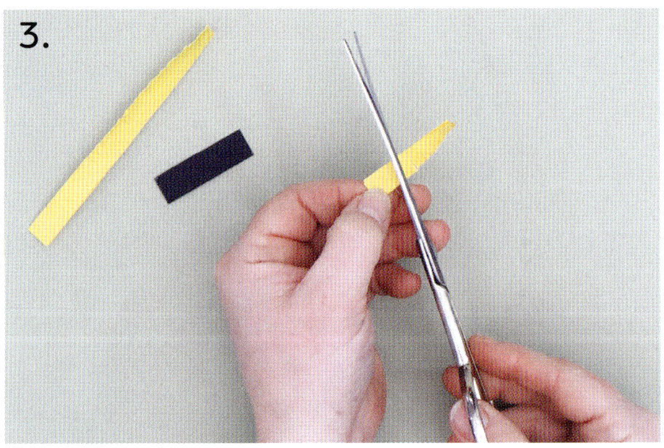
3.

4.

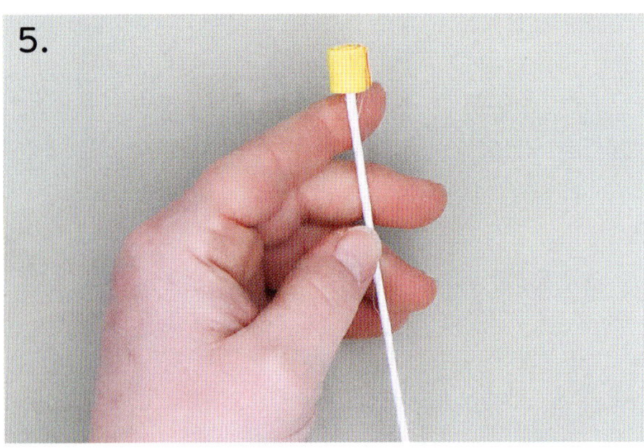
5.

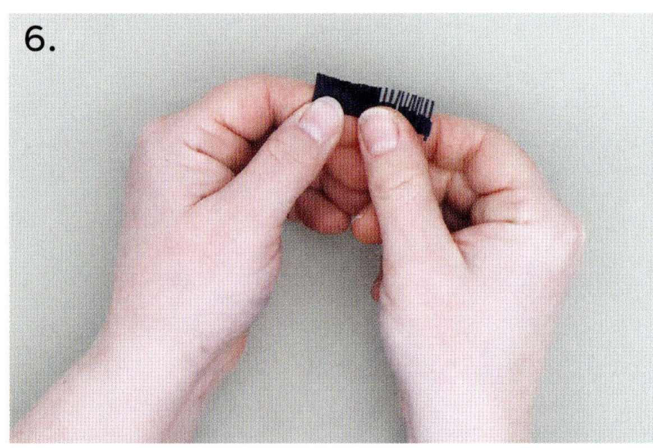
6.

7.

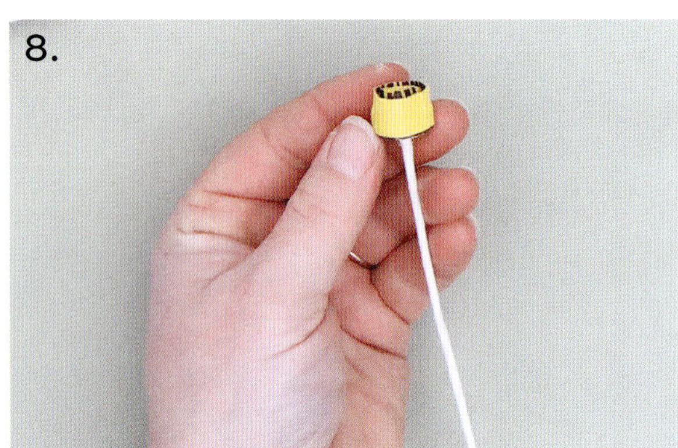
8.

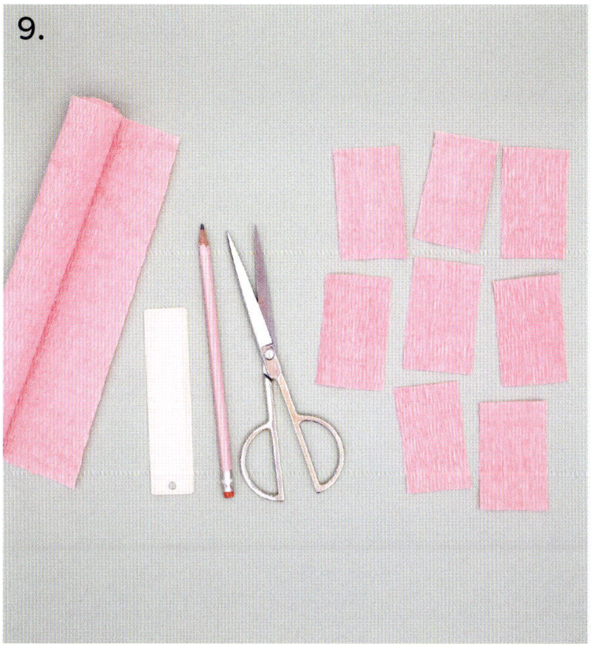

1. Start by making the centre of the cosmos. Measure and cut a rectangle ¾in (20mm) wide and 4¼in (110mm) long from the yellow cardstock.

2. Fold in half widthways so you have a ⅜in (10mm) wide and 4¼in (110mm) long rectangle. On the folded edge side, cut into the strip in small 1/32in (1mm) increments to create a frilled-edge effect.

3. Now cut one dark brown or black rectangle ⅜in (10mm) wide and 1½in (40mm) long and one yellow rectangle ¾in (20mm) wide and 1½in (40mm) long. Fold the yellow rectangle in half widthways so you have a ⅜in (10mm) wide and 1½in (40mm) long rectangle. Cut into the folded edge side of the yellow rectangle and also the black rectangle in 1/32in (1mm) or less increments to create a frilled-edge effect to both (the same as the first one).

4. Take the floristry stem wire and the largest yellow frilled rectangle. Starting at one of the short ends of the rectangle, glue the wire into position roughly halfway (¼in/5mm) into the rectangle using hot glue. Ensure the folded, frilled edge is at the top.

5. Wind the cardstock around the wire as tightly as possible, gluing to secure it as you go. Try to keep the paper at the same level to ensure you create one solid flat-topped central piece.

6. Now take the dark brown or black frilled-edge rectangle. Fold down every other frilled section so that there is a gap between each frill. This might seem fiddly, but this small adaptation will be worthwhile to create a realistic effect. The solid line of dark colouring against the yellow looks too harsh for a delicate cosmos.

7. Glue the dark brown or black frilled strip around the already attached yellow central piece, making sure the folded frills are tucked down inside.

8. Follow on with the second yellow frilled rectangle around it to complete the cosmos centre.

9. Now move on to cutting out the cosmos petals using the floristry crepe paper in your chosen colour. Begin by cutting eight rectangles 1½in (40mm) wide and 2¾in (70mm) long.

10. The bottom of the petal will be roughly ⅜in (10mm) wide, increasing to just under 1½in (40mm) wide at the top. Starting at the base, cut at a slight angle towards the top. Cosmos petals tend to have quite a varied top edge, so when going across the top cut into it slightly in a wavy shape to vary each petal, before going back down towards the bottom in a mirror image.

11.

12.

13.

14.

15.

16.

11. Fold and pleat each petal, creasing the crepe paper as you do to create additional ripples.

12. Start to glue the petals around the side of the central point, using a hot glue gun to secure them into place.

13. I find it easiest to first attach four petals, each at 90 degrees from the central point, before adding the next four between them in the gaps.

14. Once all of the petals are glued into position, grasp the flower around the central point and gently fold the petals outwards.

15. Starting at the base of the central piece, wrap floristry crepe tape around it to secure everything together and continue wrapping down the stem to cover the wire.

16. Once complete, slightly bend the flower head so the wire is slightly curved at the top. Tweak and re-pleat the petals, if necessary; cosmos can often be quite varied and not uniform in their appearance. You are now finished! A simple, but beautiful cosmos.

Tulip

Tulipa

Tulips are definitely one of my go-to flowers for a cheerful bunch of colour! These are very easy to make, and with a simple twist technique, they make for an effective paper flower creation. I lived briefly in Amsterdam and used to love visiting the Bloemenmarkt for floral inspiration. Making paper tulips reminds me of those happy times, and I hope they make you smile, too.

Materials

- Floristry crepe paper (your choice of colour, for the petals)
- Green floristry crepe paper (for the leaves)
- Flower pips (optional)
- Paper-covered floristry wire, roughly 16 gauge
- Dark green floristry crepe tape
- Hot glue

Tools

- Paper scissors
- Wire cutters
- Hot glue gun
- Ruler (optional)
- Pencil (optional)

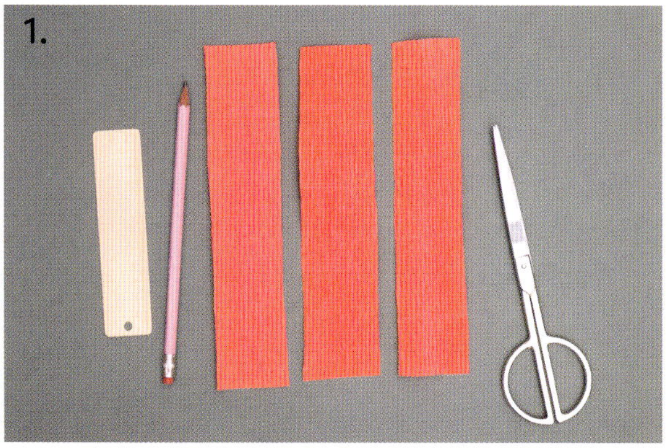
1.

2.

3.

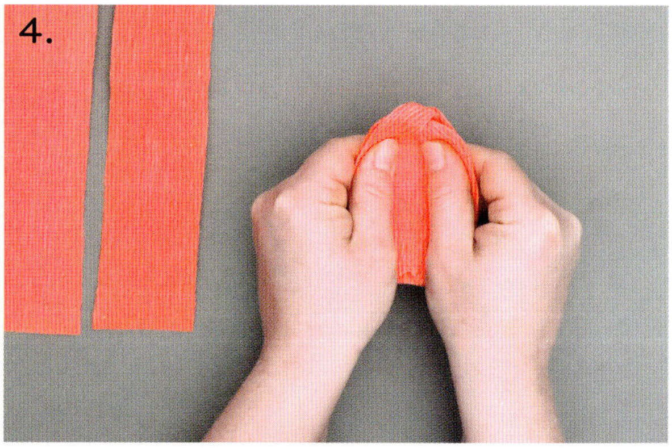
4.

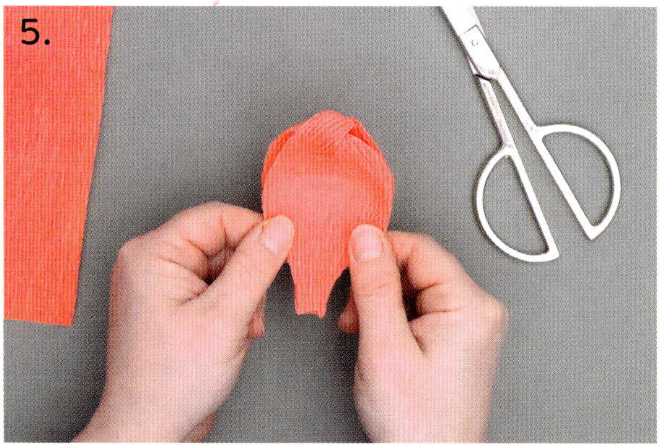
5.

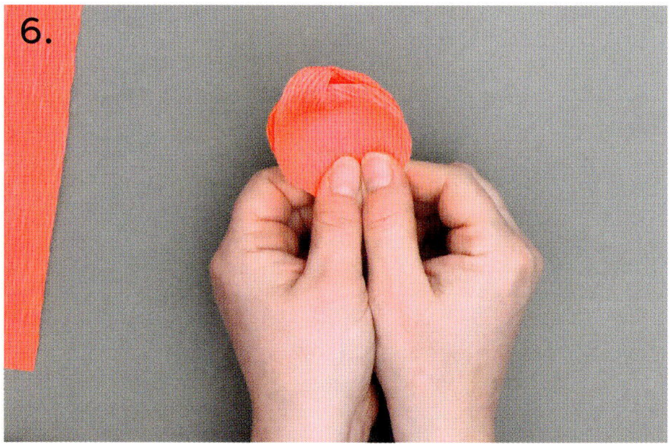
6.

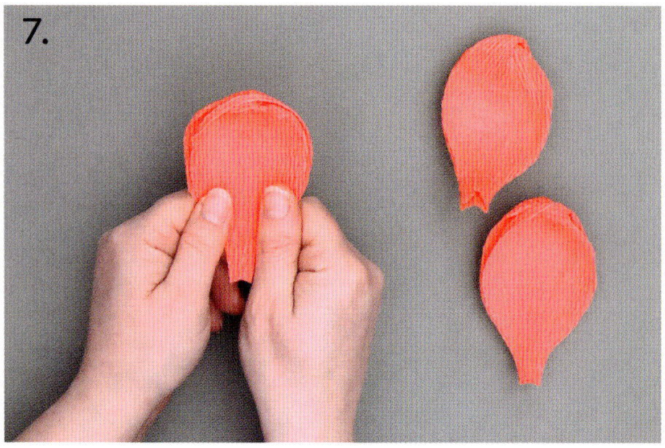
7.

8.

9.

10.

11.

12.

1. Start by making the petals for the tulip. Measure and cut three rectangles 1½in (40mm) wide and 8in (200mm) long from the floristry crepe paper. You will need the grain of the paper going along the length of each rectangle.

2. Find the middle of one of the rectangles, then twist the paper completely around so half of it faces the opposite direction.

3. Where the paper is twisted, fold it back down so the two halves are layered, one on top of the other.

4. Using your thumbs, gently push into the centre of the two layers of crepe paper to create a curve.

5. Next, shape the petals. Leaving a small base of roughly ⅜in (10mm) wide at the bottom, cut into both layers, curving just upwards on each side. Don't go around the top: you need to keep the twisted layers together. Think of the petals almost as having a hot-air balloon shape.

6. Using the glue gun, add a small amount of glue between each layer so they stick together.

7. Repeat steps 2–6 with the other two rectangles.

8. If you would like to add flower pips (this is an optional step), do so now. Fold the three double-ended flower pips in half. Using the floristry crepe tape, secure them to the very tip of the paper-covered wire. If you are not using flower pips, move on to step 9.

9. Attach one of the petals to the stem wire using floristry crepe tape to secure.

10. Repeat with the second petal, moving around the wire stem.

11. Finally, add the last petal in the same way.

12. Wrap the floristry crepe paper around the stem to completely cover it.

13.

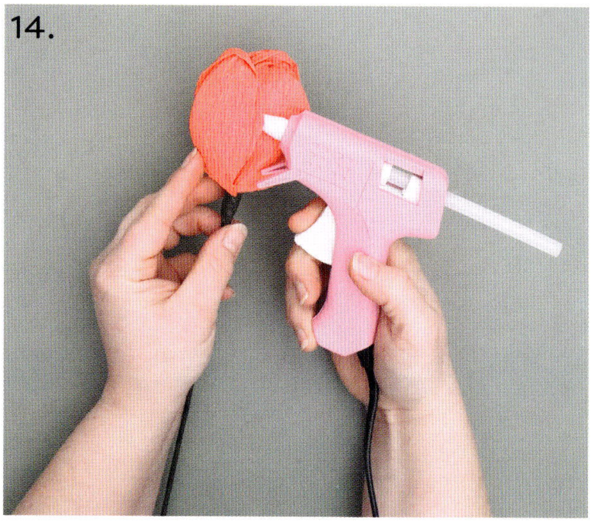
14.

15.

16.

17.

18.

13. Now, don't be afraid to give the petals a really good squeeze downwards – it helps to push the sides outwards and recreate that naturally bulbous look of tulips!

14. If you find the petals are not staying close together or are splaying outwards, use the glue gun with just a small amount of glue between the petals to fix them into position.

15. The tulip stem is complete – now turn your attention to adding some leaves.

Leaves

16. From the green floristry crepe paper, cut two rectangles 1⅛–1½in (30–40mm) wide and 9½in (240mm) long. Now cut the the rectangles into elongated almond shapes.

17. Gently bend the leaves to curve them.

18. Using the floristry crepe tape, attach the leaves about halfway down and on either side of the stem. And there, you have a beautiful tulip!

Japanese Anemone

Anemone hupehensis

These beautiful flowers sway gently in the late summer breeze each year in our neighbour's front garden. They always look so elegant and inspiring. They are an absolute pleasure to both look at and create from paper! The flowers themselves are quick to make and this project offers a good technique to create the stamens, which you could use in other projects too. In this technique, the grain direction of the floristry crepe paper is used to replicate the fabulously textured centre.

Materials

- White or pink floristry crepe paper (for the stamens and petals)
- Yellow or peach floristry crepe paper (for the stamens)
- Green floristry crepe paper (for the leaves and buds)
- Green ⅜in (10mm) woollen felt balls
- Paper-covered floristry wire, roughly 16 gauge
- Dark green floristry crepe tape
- Hot glue

Tools

- Paper scissors
- Wire cutters
- Glue gun
- Ruler
- Pencil

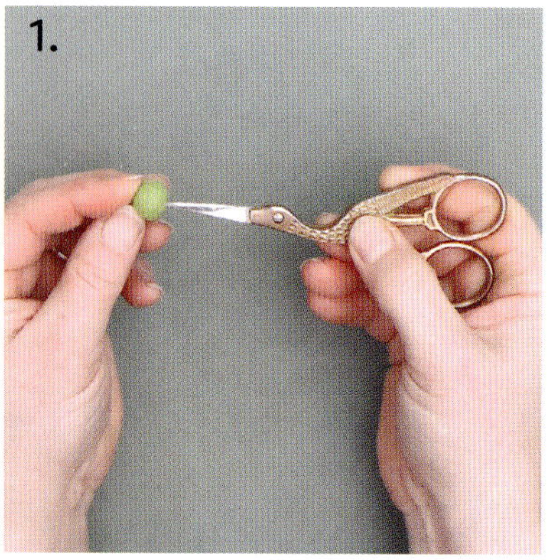
1.

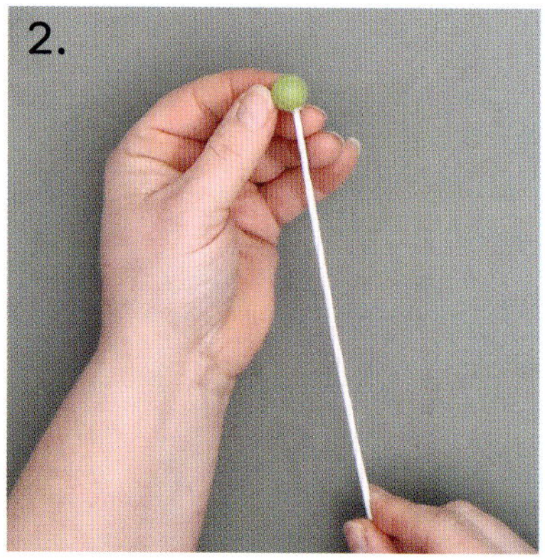
2.

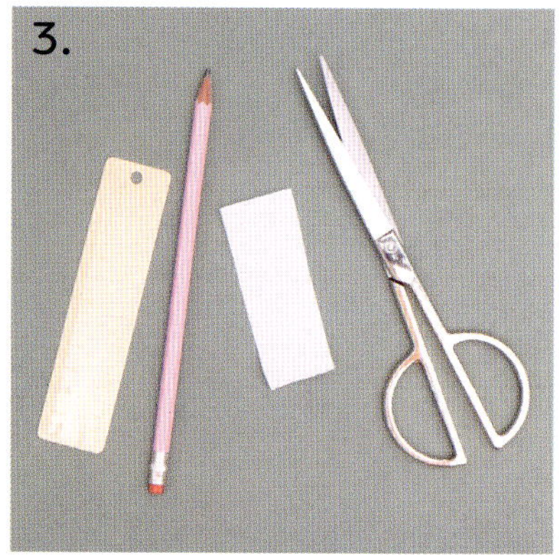
3.

4.

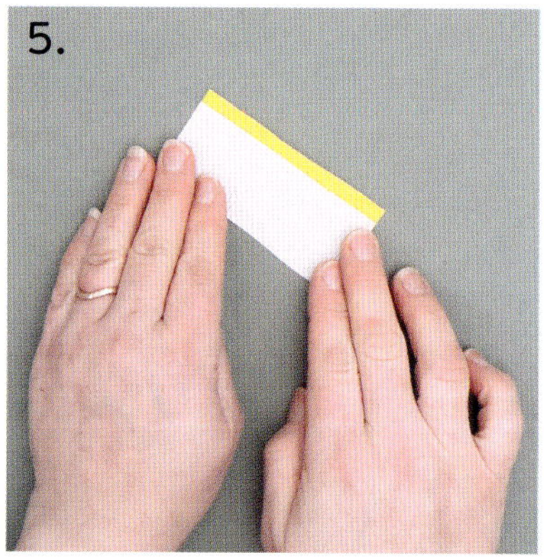
5.

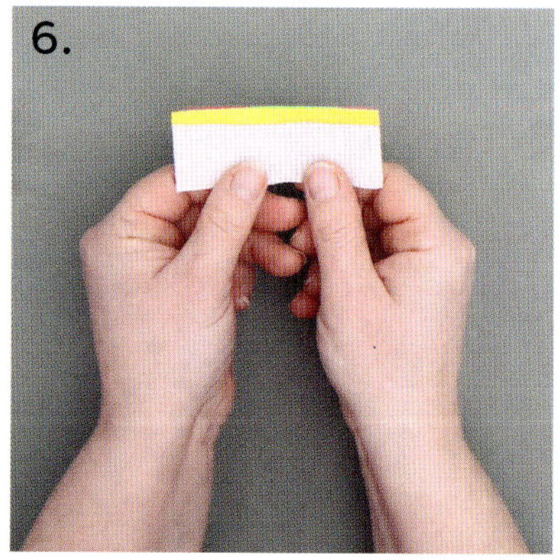
6.

7.

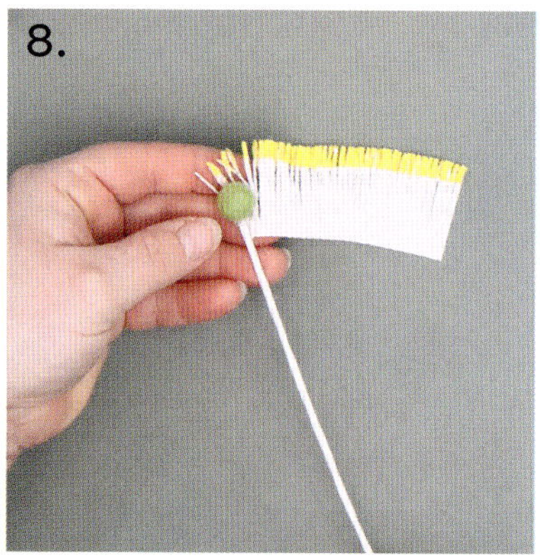
8.

9.

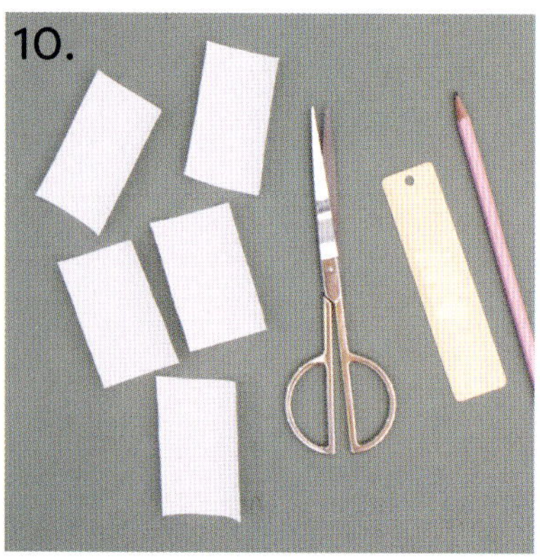
10.

11.

12.

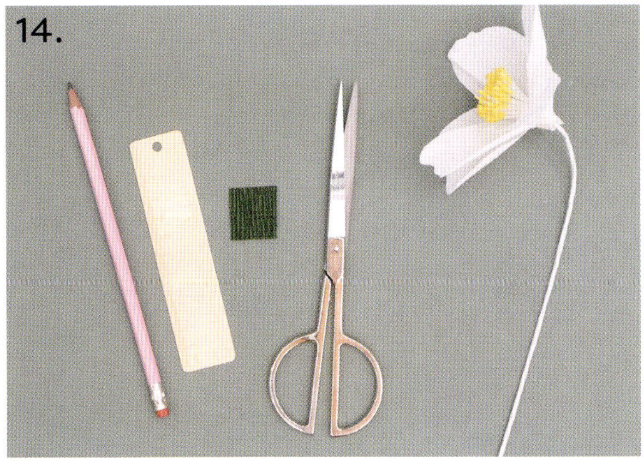

Flower

1. Using a tapestry sewing needle or sharp embroidery scissors, gently and carefully insert the sharp tip into the woollen felt ball to make a small hole halfway through. This will make a space to add the stem wire.

2. Add a small amount of glue to the tip of the wire before inserting it into the hole in the felt ball.

3. To make the stamens, cut a rectangle from the white floristry paper 1⅛in (30mm) wide and 3⅛in (80mm) long. You will need the grain of the paper to run along the width of the rectangle.

4. Cut a rectangle ⅜in (10mm) wide and 3⅛in (80mm) long from the yellow or peach floristry crepe. The paper grain should run along the length of the rectangle.

5. Place the long white rectangle on top of the yellow rectangle, halfway up the height. Glue it into place to secure it, making sure there is a thin layer of glue all the way across.

6. Fold the yellow down over the edge of your white rectangle and glue into position. Your white rectangle edge will be enclosed inside, surrounded by your yellow rectangle on both sides. Allow your glue to fully dry before moving on to Step 7.

7. Along the long yellow edge, cut into the strip in small increments to create a frilled effect, cutting through the yellow and into the white section. Take care not to cut all the way through, making sure there is an uncut band at the base.

8. To attach to the stem, place the felt ball roughly halfway up the paper near a short end and gently glue it around with the hot glue gun. Since some varieties of Japanese anemone have many more stamens, you could make and add a second layer of stamens if you prefer a fuller centre.

9. Gently press open the stamens away from the central felt ball.

10. Next, make the petals. Most Japanese anemones have five petals, but some varieties have more. To begin, cut five rectangles from the floristry crepe paper 2in (50mm) wide and 2¾in (70mm) long. You want the grain of the crepe to run up the height of each rectangle.

11. To cut the shape of the petals, start with a small base at the bottom and make a curved cut that is much wider around the side and rounder at the top before repeating the other side. It should be similar to a hot-air balloon shape. Try to vary the top of each petal, so they are slightly irregular – some could have small notches or curved indentations to create variety.

12. Attach the base of each petal to the base of the felt ball/stamens with the hot glue.

13. Working your way around, attach each one evenly around the centre.

14. Once all the petals are attached, cut a ¾in (20mm) square from the green floristry crepe paper.

15.

16.

17.

18.
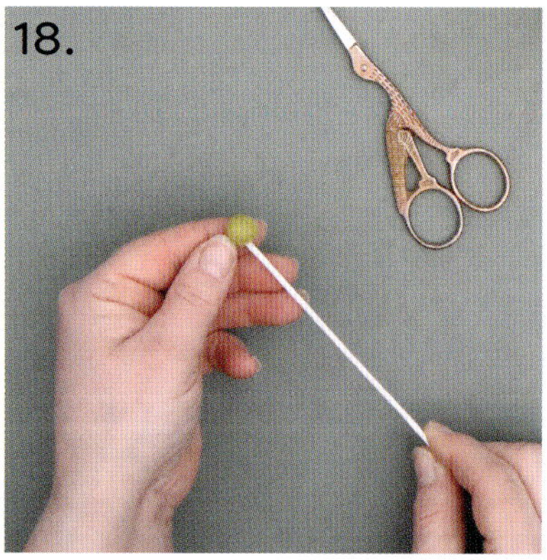

19.

20.

21.

22.

23.

24.

25.

26.

You could use the flower stem on its own, or since Japanese anemones are often multi-stem plants, you can make additional bud stems to combine together. If you wish to do this, you will need additional paper-covered floristry wire as well as green ⅜in (10mm) woollen felt balls.

15. Stretch the green square and glue it around the base of the flower to secure the ends of all of the petals. Some of the green will spread down the stem – it will be concealed in the next step.

16. Use the floristry crepe tape to cover the excess green paper and wrap it around the stem to completely cover it.

17. Bend the flower head at a 90-degree angle as close to the base of the flower as possible. Ruffle the petals a little if needed to make it not look too pristine! You can now use the flower stem as it is or continue to add buds and additional flowers to make it a multi-stem flower.

Bud

18. Using a wire stem shorter than the main stem, and a felt ball, repeat steps 1 and 2 to attach the felt ball to the wire.

19. Next, use the floristry crepe tape to completely cover each stem from the base of the felt ball, all the way down to the bottom.

20. Slightly bend the wire in the middle to make the bud sit at an unusual angle. Set aside.

Leaves

21. Making one or two leaves per multi-stem, cut one 3½in (90mm) square of green paper per leaf.

22. To create a simple three-part leaf shape, fold the square in half. Starting from the folded edge side, from the bottom, cut up in a 45-degree angle towards the side before curving back round to the middle. Then go back up towards the top before cutting into the folded edge side. This sounds more complicated than it is, and folding the square in half will allow you to cut the leaf symmetrically.

23. Open the leaf outwards. Along the very edges of the leaf, make small snips every ¼in (5mm) or so.

24. Gently pull at the edges to open out these snips. This will provide a serrated edge finish.

Assembly

25. Anemone stems can include several buds, multiple flowers and a number of leaves. You can adapt your flower to however you want the stem to appear, but if making a vase of the same variety, try to mix up each stem to have a different number of buds and flowers to create a natural look. Two flowers, one bud and two leaves are being used for this project.

26. Arrange the flowers to meet at a central point. Ensure the flowers curve at irregular angles. You can adapt the angles at a later stage, but it helps to adjust them now to visualize how the final stem will look. Wrap the floristry crepe tape around all of the combined stems to secure them. Next attach the bud.

27. At the point where the stems meet, add the leaves, using hot glue at the base of each leaf to attach them. Position one leaf pointing out towards the back, and mirror the other on the opposite side facing towards you. Finished! You have a lovely Japanese anemone.

French Marigold

Tagetes patula

There are many varieties of marigolds in a myriad of vibrant oranges, reds and yellows – with all those sunny petals, it is such a cheerful flower! This project may seem complex due to the number of petals to cut, but the assembly is simple and the flowers can be made relatively quickly.

Materials

- Orange floristry crepe paper (for the petals)
- Green floristry crepe paper (for the sepals)
- Paper-covered floristry wire, roughly 16 gauge
- Dark green floristry crepe tape
- Hot glue

Tools

- Paper scissors
- Wire cutters
- Glue gun
- Ruler (optional)
- Pencil (optional)

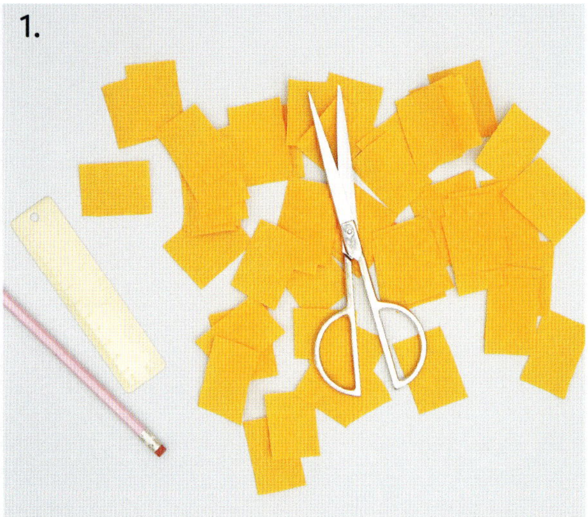
1.

2.

3.

4.

5.

6.

1. Start making the petals from the orange floristry crepe paper by cutting 70 rectangles 1⅛in (30mm) wide and 1½in (40mm) long. Keep the grain running up the height of the rectangles.

2. Now shape the petals. Starting at the narrow base of the petal, cut upwards diagonally before cutting across the top with a wiggly varied edge. Go back down diagonally on the other side back to the base. You can cut two petals at a time if you like!

3. Begin to attach the petals to the stem wire. First make pleats in one of the petals to create a small ruffle. Place it with roughly ⅜in (10mm) of the base of the petal on the end of the wire, then use the green floristry crepe tape to secure it.

4. Continue to attach petals in this way, pleating and attaching, working your way around the stem until you have added 20 petals.

5. Now switch to using hot glue to attach petals. Continue to work your way around the the centre, but now attaching petals unpleated and flat. Tease the petals outwards slightly from the top to create a blooming effect.

6. Keep attaching petals, moving your way around the flower until all 70 petals are secured.

7. To make the sepal, cut a rectangle from the green crepe 1⅛in (30mm) wide and 2⅜in (60mm) long. The grain needs to run up the height of the sepal.

8. Stretch the crepe paper and glue it around the base of the marigold to conceal the ends of the petals, twisting it down onto your stem wire.

9. Secure the sepal in place on the stem with the green floristry tape, and continue to wrap the tape down the stem to entirely cover it.

TIP
To make a slightly bigger French marigold, simply continue to add more petals. Or, start with slightly larger petals. If you are making a bunch of marigolds, it would be good to vary the size slightly to add to the natural effect.

Buttercup

Ranunculus bulbosus

Is it a wildflower, or is it a weed? However you would like to classify it, this golden beauty is such a delicate little flower. It also has another name: St Anthony's turnip! It may not have the biggest blossoms, but the cheery flower heads are effective when displayed on a few stems in a bud vase.

Materials

- Yellow cardstock, 150gsm or less (for the petals)
- Yellow floristry crepe paper (for the centre)
- Pale green floristry crepe paper (for the centre)
- Green floristry crepe paper (for the leaves)
- Thin green floristry stub wire, roughly 22 gauge
- Pale green floristry crepe tape
- Hot glue
- PVA glue

Tools

- Paper scissors
- Wire cutters
- Paintbrush
- Glue gun
- Ruler (optional)
- Pencil (optional)

1.

2.

3.

4.

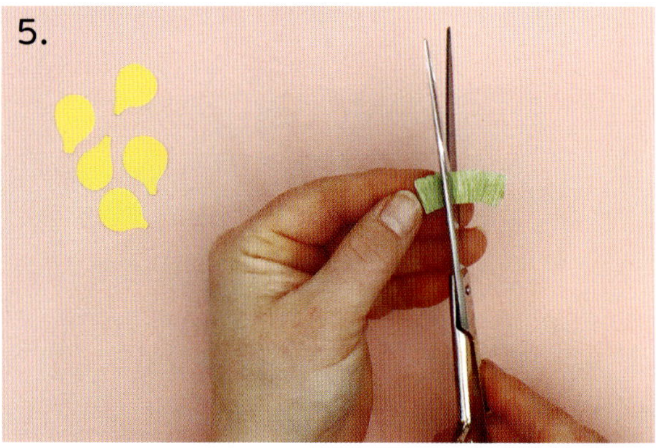
5.

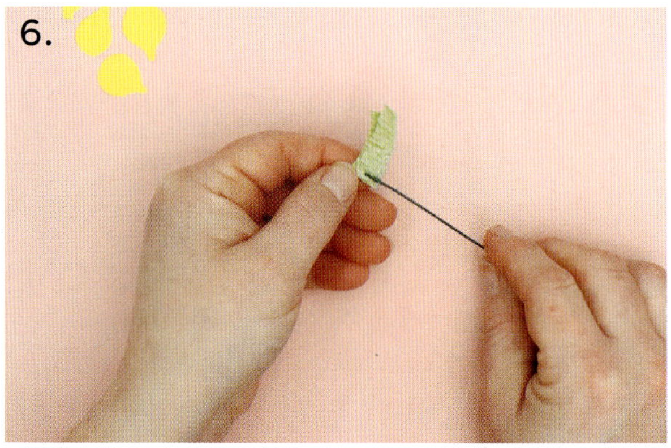
6.

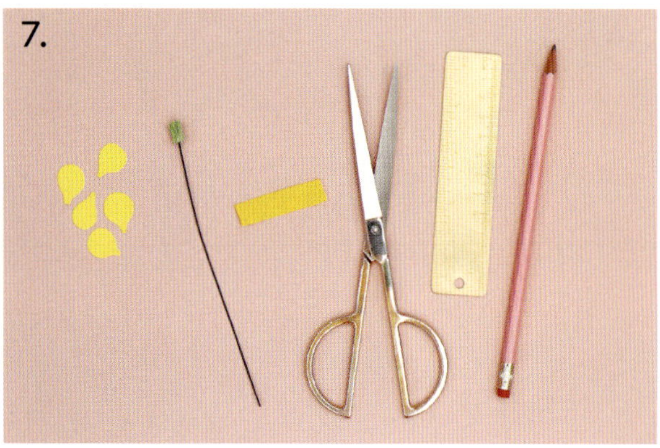
7.

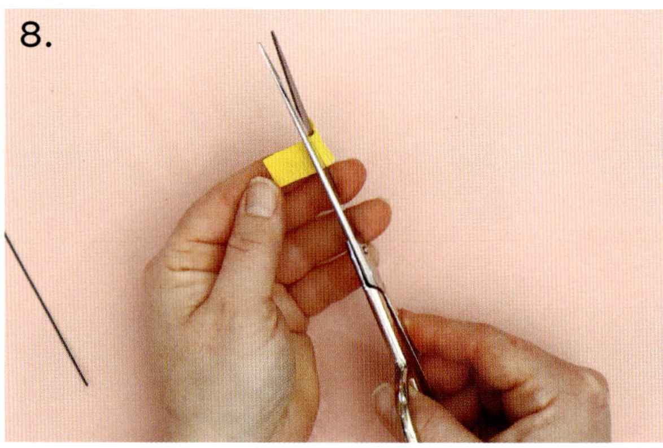
8.

1. Using the paintbrush, apply a light coat of PVA glue on the yellow cardstock. Leave to dry. (The glue coating gives the petals a luscious and glossy look.)

2. Once dry, cut five roughly ¾in (20mm) squares.

3. Cut each square into an almost hot-air balloon shape, with a narrow base and a larger circular petal above. Set aside.

4. Cut a ¾in (20mm) square from the pale green floristry crepe paper.

5. Fold the square in half, with the crepe grain running upwards. Cut into the strip along the folded edge in 1/32in (1mm) or less increments to create a frilled effect. Take care not to cut all the way through, leaving an uncut band at the base.

6. Now, starting at a short end of the rectangle, hot glue a piece of the floristry stub wire in place roughly halfway into the rectangle. Ensure the folded, frilled edge is at the top. Wind the crepe paper around the stem.

7. Cut a rectangle from the yellow floristry crepe paper, ⅜in (10mm) wide and 2in (50mm) long, with the grain running along the width of the rectangle.

8. Now cut into the strip on the folded side in 1/32in (1mm) or less increments to create a frilled effect. Wind it around the existing green centre, making sure the bottom edges of the strips are lined up.

9. Glue one of the yellow cardstock petals onto the central piece. Keep the glue at the very base of the petal.

10. Continue to add the remaining petals, ensuring they are an even height around the centre, until all they are all attached.

11. Use the green floristry crepe paper to make a sepal, which will conceal the petal ends and form the base of the buttercup. Cut five elongated almond shapes. The ones I have cut are just over ⅜in (10mm) wide and ¾in (20mm) long.

12. Glue the sepal pieces to the base of the flower, halfway up the petals and slightly down the stem.

13.

TIP
You can stop at step 13 and make this single stem or you can continue and make a multi-stem version.

14.

15.

16.

17.

18.

13. Once all the sepals are attached, using the floristry crepe tape, cover the base of the sepal and continue to wrap it around the wire to completely cover the stem.

14. Make two further flowers, repeating steps 1–13.

15. Position two of the flowers together, keeping the flower heads at a similar height, and use the floristry crepe tape to join them at their stems.

16. Now add small upper leaves. Cut two elongated almond shapes from the green floristry crepe paper, making them roughly 1½in (40mm) long.

17. Place the leaves at the join where the two stems meet, then secure them in place by wrapping some additional floristry crepe tape around them.

18. You now have two flowers on the same stem. Move further downwards, and repeat steps 15–17 to attach the final third buttercup. Bend the stems slightly to add a natural look to the buttercups. And you are finished! You could attach more flowers if you wanted to, depending on how you wish to use the stem.

Chrysanthemum

Chrysanthemum indicum

This beautifully versatile flower is a classic staple bloom for bouquets. This project allows you to make different versions at every stage of growth, from small buds up to larger full blooms. When combined, they make a lovely natural mixed bunch.

Materials

- Cardstock, A4 (letter) size and 150gsm or less (your choice of colour, for the petals)
- Green or brown 9/16in (15mm) woollen felt ball
- Paper-covered floristry wire, roughly 16 gauge
- Green floristry crepe tape
- Green floristry crepe paper (for the sepal)
- Hot glue

Tools

- Paper scissors
- Wire cutters
- Tapestry needle or sharp embroidery scissors
- Hot glue gun
- Ruler (optional)
- Pencil (optional)

1.

2.

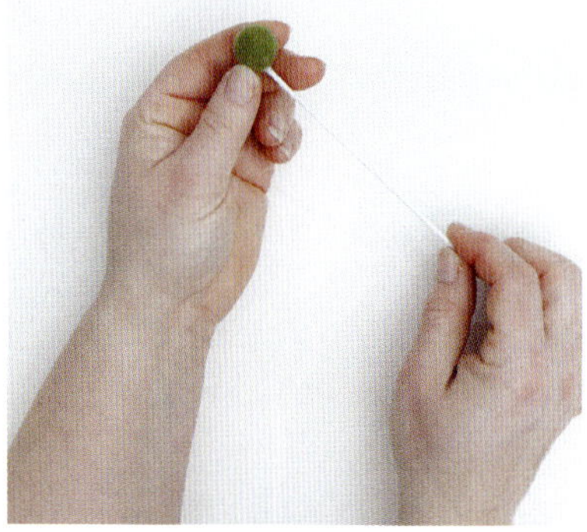

3.

4.

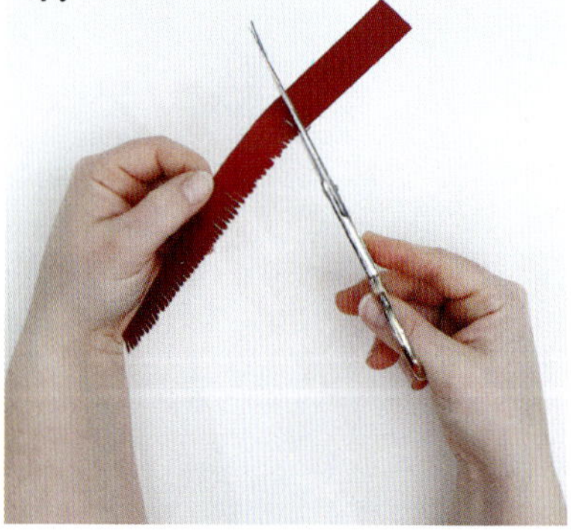

5.

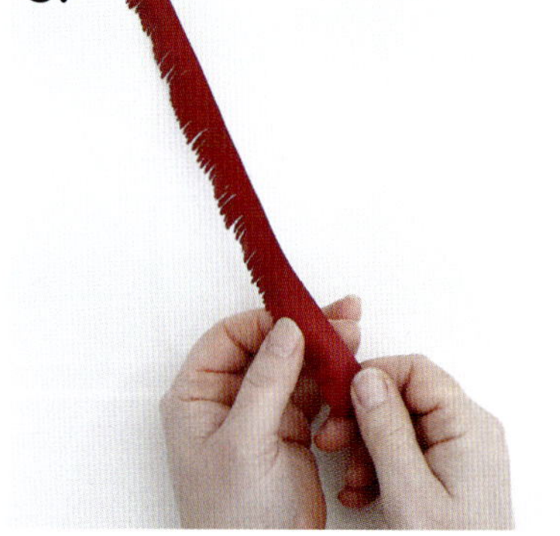

6.

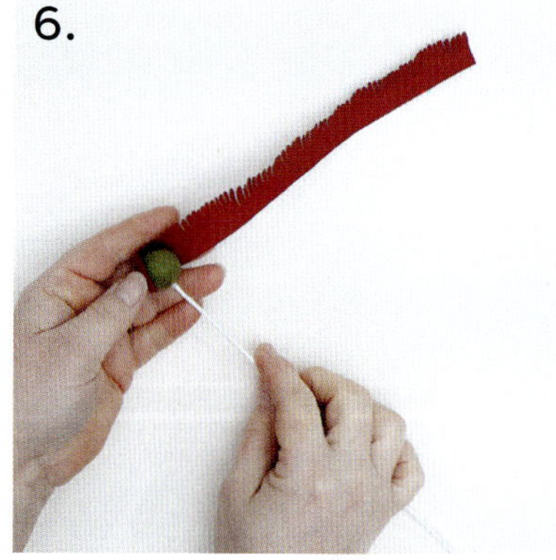

7.

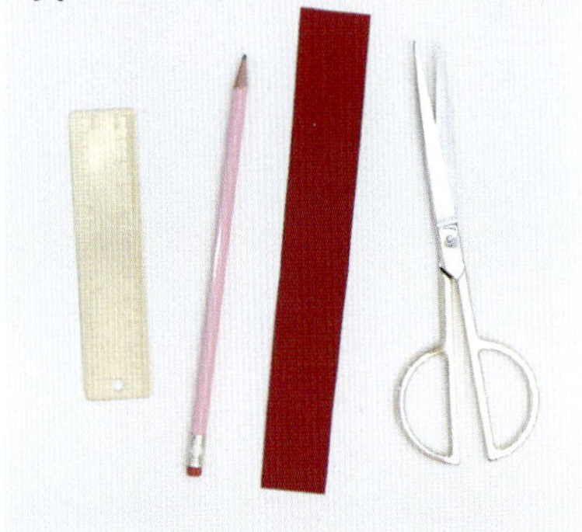

8.

9.

10.

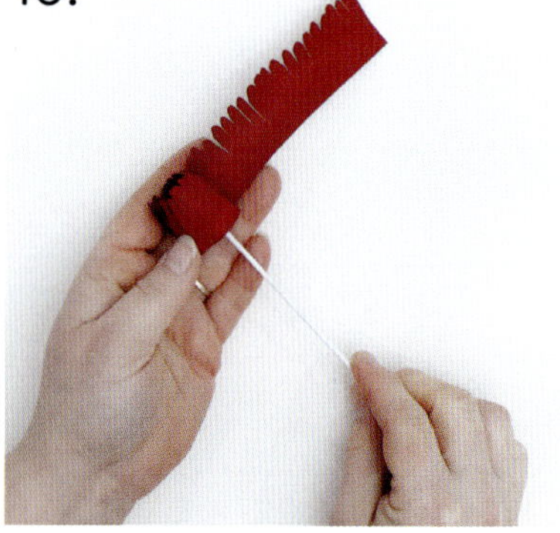

11.

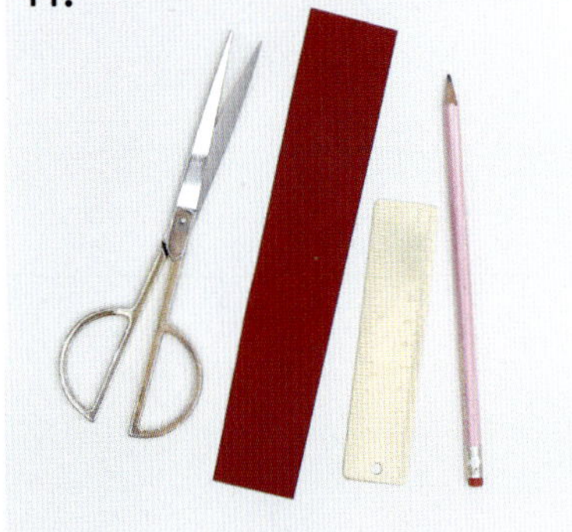

12.

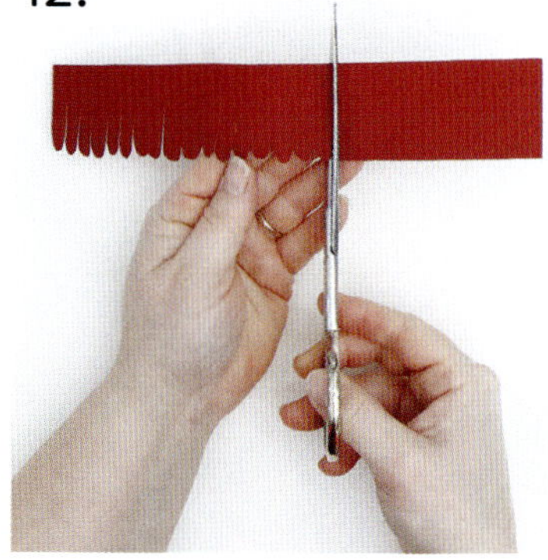

13.

14.

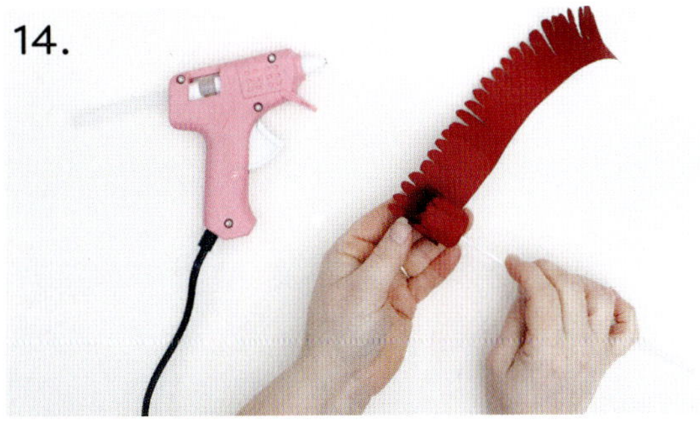

To make the centre

1. Using a tapestry sewing needle or sharp embroidery scissors, carefully insert the tip into the woollen felt ball to make a small hole, going roughly halfway through. It will make space for the stem wire.

2. Add a small dab of glue to the tip of the stem wire, then insert it into the opening in the ball to secure.

To make a bud

Note: do steps 1–2 for the centre of the flower before moving on to this stage.

3. From the cardstock for the petals, cut a rectangle 9⁄16–¾in (15–20mm) wide and 8¼in (210mm) long.

4. Cut into the rectangle in ⅛–5⁄32in (3–4mm) increments, giving each part a curved top edge. Take care not to cut all the way through, leaving an uncut band at the base. Try to keep each petal roughly the same height and size.

5. Using your fingers or a pencil, curl the petals over slightly so they point inwards.

6. Use hot glue to secure the cardstock strip to the felt ball centre, with the curved side against the ball. Wind the strip around the ball, allowing a small gap at the centre so you can see the felt.

Note: if making only a bud, skip ahead to steps 23–26 to make the base and finish the flower.

To make a small flower

Note: do steps 1–6 for the centre and bud before moving on to this next stage.

7. From the cardstock for the petals, cut a rectangle 1⅛in (30mm) wide and 8¼in (210mm) long.

8. Cut into the rectangle in ⅛–¼in (3–5mm) increments, giving each part a curved top edge. Take care not to cut all the way through, leaving an uncut band at the base. Try to keep each petal roughly the same height and size.

9. Using your fingers or a pencil, curl the petals over slightly so they point inwards.

10. Use hot glue to secure the strip to the centre, winding it around the bud.

Note: if making only a small flower, skip ahead to steps 23–26 to make the base and finish the flower.

To make a medium flower

Note: do steps 1–10 for the centre, bud and small flower before moving on to this stage.

11. From the cardstock for the petals, cut a rectangle 1½in (40mm) wide and 8¼in (210mm) long.

12. Cut into the rectangle in roughly ¼in (5mm) increments, giving each part a curved top edge. Take care not to cut all the way through, leaving an uncut band at the base. Try to keep each petal roughly the same height and size.

13. Using your fingers or a pencil, curl the petals over slightly, but this time curve them so they are pointing outwards.

14. Use hot glue to secure the strip to the centre, winding it around the small flower.

Note: if making only a medium flower, skip ahead to steps 23–26 to make the base and finish the flower.

15.

16.

17.

18.

19.

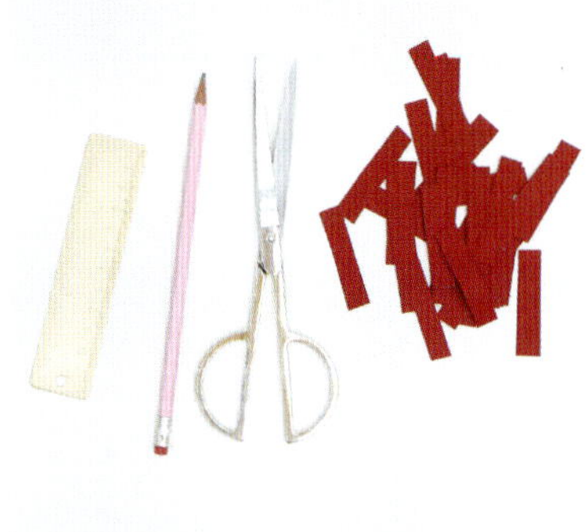

20.

21.

22.

23.

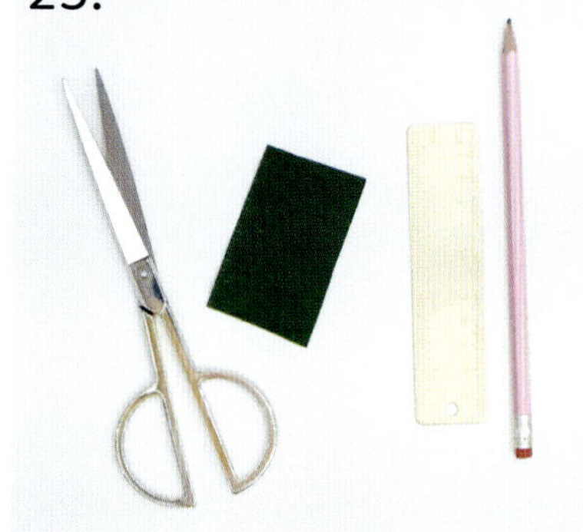

24.

25.

26.

To make a large flower

Note: do steps 1–14, for the centre, bud, and small and medium flowers, before moving on to this stage.

15. From the cardstock for the petals, cut two rectangles 1½in (40mm) wide and 8¼in (210mm) long.

16. Cut into the rectangles in roughly ¼in (5mm) increments, giving each part a curved top edge. Take care not to cut all the way through, leaving an uncut band at the base. Try to keep each petal roughly the same height and size.

17. Using your fingers or a pencil, curl the petals over slightly with the curved shape pointing outwards.

18. Use hot glue to secure the two strips to the centre, winding them around the medium flower.

Note: if making only a large flower, skip ahead to steps 23–26 to make the base and finish the flower.

To make an extra large flower

Note: do steps 1–18, from the centre, bud and through to the large flower, before moving on to this stage.

19. Cut 35 individual rectangles and ¼–⅜in (5–10mm) wide and 2in (50mm) long. You can add even more petals if you wish, so feel free to continue and experiment for a larger flower.

20. Cut the rectangles into a shape that is curved at the top and slightly thinner at the bottom.

21. Glue the petals onto the large flower, moving your way around so they are attached evenly.

22. Gently tease out the petals so the flower is more open and blooming.

For the base

23. Once you get to this size, the back width of your chrysanthemum can become quite wide, but we will now cut some green floristry paper to secure the back of your bloom. In amongst a bouquet, you won't notice the back width so much. Cut a piece of green floristry paper to secure the base of the bloom. Use one of these dimensions, depending on the size of the flower. The direction of the grain should run along the paper width.

    Bud: 1⅛in (30mm) square
    Small: 1⅛in (30mm) wide and 1½in (40mm) long
    Medium: 1½in (40mm) wide and 2in (50mm) long
    Large: 1½in (40mm) wide and 2⅜in (60mm) long
    Extra large bloom: 1½in (40mm) wide and 2¾in (70mm) long

24. Stretch the square or rectangle, then glue it around the very bottom of the flower base.

25. Twist any excess green floristry paper up underneath the flower before securing it with the floristry crepe tape.

26. Continue to wrap the floristry crepe tape to cover the entire stem. You are now finished! A beautiful chrysanthemum.

Clematis

Clematis viticella

There are nearly 400 varieties of this vibrant plant. We have a beautiful purple clematis that grows crazily every summer around our front door. While I wouldn't usually pick any of our live flowers, the benefit of this paper project is that you can create and use these large flowers however you like. They would be great wrapped around a wreath or as a garland project. Alternatively, you could attach them individually to a wire stem to include in a bouquet.

Materials

- Floristry crepe paper (your choice of colour, for the petals)
- White or pale yellow floristry crepe paper (for the centre)
- Green floristry crepe paper (for the leaves)
- Paper-covered floristry wire, roughly 16 gauge
- Floristry stub wire, roughly 20 gauge
- Dark green floristry crepe tape
- Hot glue

Tools

- Paper scissors
- Wire cutters
- Glue gun
- Ruler & pencil (optional)

1.
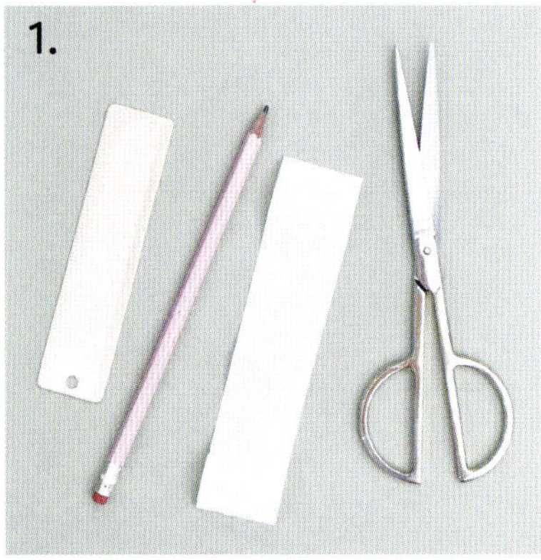

2.
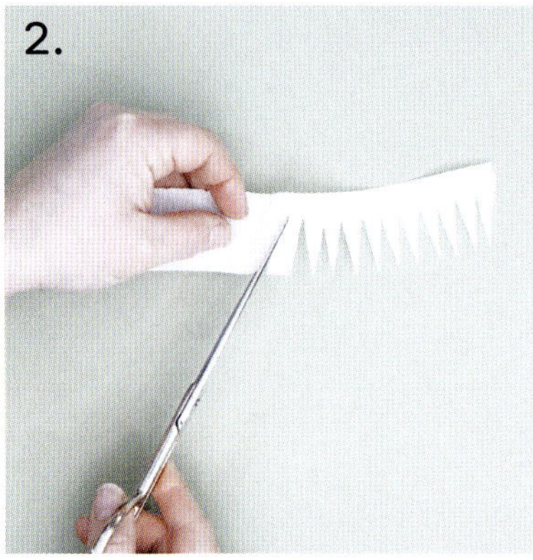

3.

4.

5.

6.

7.

8.

9.

10.

1. From the white floristry crepe paper, cut a rectangle 1⅛–1½in (30–40mm) wide and 6¼in (160mm) long. The wider you make it, the longer the centre will be. You will need the grain of the paper to go along the width of the rectangle.

2. Cut large zigzags into this white paper roughly ⅜in (10mm) wide and ¾–1⅛in (20–30mm) long. You need between 16 and 20 triangular points across the white length, depending on how wide you make each one.

3. Twist each of these triangles with your fingers to make them thin and spindly.

4. To make the clematis centre, cut the paper-covered floristry wire to roughly 2¾in (70mm) and wind the paper around it, using hot glue to secure it.

5. Tease out some of the white parts so some stay central and some are much further outwards. Some clematis varieties have much larger centres, so feel free to add a second round if you like.

6. Now make petals from the floristry crepe paper. Some clematis have six petals, but this version has four – feel free to increase the petals if you wish. Cut four rectangles 2¾ (70mm) wide and 4¾in (120mm) long. Keep the grain of the paper running up the height of the rectangles.

7. Cut one of these rectangles diagonally so you have two triangles.

8. Turn one of the triangles over: you will see the grain now meets in the middle. Ensure that the grain runs downwards into an upright 'V' shape – not as an upside down 'V'.

9. Run a small amount of hot glue along the central diagonal edge of one of the triangles, before placing the other triangle on top, just slightly overlapping them.

10. Repeat steps 7–9 with the other rectangles.

11. Cut the rectangles into petal shapes, starting at the base (with the point of the 'V' shape in the grain towards you). Make the petal narrow for ¾–1⅛in (20–30mm), then cut it into a wider curve and back to a point at the top, then cut a mirror image on the other side. The petals will be roughly 2–2⅜in (50–60mm) wide and 4¼–4¾in (110–120mm) long.

12. When all the petals are cut out, begin gluing them on. Using hot glue, attach the base of each petal to the central piece and work your way evenly around it.

13. Using either a pencil or your fingers, shape each petal so it is slightly curved in the middle.

14.

15.

16.

17.

18.

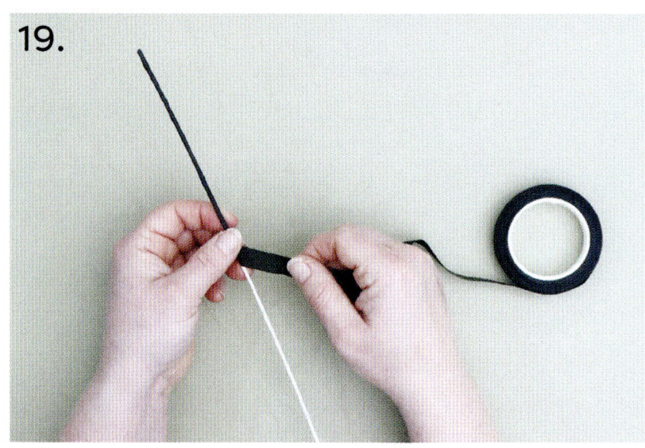
19.

20.

21.

14. Use the crepe tape to cover the back of the clematis and secure the petals into position, then wrap it completely down the stem.

15. To make clematis leaves from the green floristry crepe paper, cut rectangles 3⅛in (80mm) wide and 4¾in (120mm) long. Repeat steps 7–8 to cut triangles and form leaves with the grain in a 'V'.

16. Place a piece of thin stub wire cut slightly longer than the leaves at the centre of each one. (This will allow you to really curve the leaves.) Glue the triangles together as in step 9, including the wire.

17. Cut the leaves into shapes similar to the petals, but make the base part slightly wider. Take care when cutting the leaf near the wire (use the wire cutters if needed). The leaves will be roughly 2–2⅜in (50–60mm) wide and 4¾in (120mm) long.

18. Cover the very base of the leaf and any visible stem wire with the floristry crepe tape. Slightly curve the leaf using the wire as an aid.

19. You can now use the flowers and leaves however you wish. For this project, they are assembled into a garland. For a stem, cover a length of paper-covered floristry stem wire with floristry crepe tape, wrapping it around to entirely cover it.

20. Use the floristry crepe tape to attach the flowers and leaves to the stem wire.

21. Attach as many flowers and leaves as you like! Try to keep them pointing in different directions for a natural look. If you want to make an even longer garland, you could join stems together to keep the clematis growing much further!

Carnation

Dianthus caryophyllus

There is something so lovely and delicate about the classic carnation. It is the official birth flower for January, but this flower is actually available all year round. These paper ones would be wonderful mixed in bouquets for adding colour and texture, and they are beautiful as buttonholes – this simple little flower is such a versatile bloom!

Materials

- Floristry crepe paper (your choice of colour, for the petals)
- Green floristry crepe paper (optional)
- Paper-covered floristry wire, roughly 16 gauge
- Pale green floristry crepe tape

Tools

- Paper scissors
- Wire cutters
- Ruler
- Pencil

1.

2.

3.

4.

5.

6.

1. Start by cutting 20 rectangles roughly 1½in (40mm) wide and 2⅜in (60mm) long from the floristry crepe paper. Keep the grain running along the height of the rectangles. These petals may seem long for a small carnation, but some of the length will create the naturally occurring bulbous base behind the frilly petals.

2. Next, cut them into their shapes. Allow for a narrow base before cutting wider towards the top corner, then cut along the top with a small zigzag finish before going back down the other side in a mirror image. Try to vary the zigzag shape so the petals are not all perfect. Some varieties have more of a zigzag edge than others, so experiment with how you would like these to look.

3. Now start attaching the petals to the stem wire. Take one of the petals and pleat it to create a small ruffled petal. Place the stem wire in the petal with the wire roughly halfway up the petal height.

4. Attach the petal to the wire using the pale green floristry crepe tape.

5. Repeat with a further four petals in the same way, moving around the centre.

6. For the next petal, add it on flat, without pleating, using more floristry tape to secure it.

7. Continue to add the rest of the petals in the same way, moving around the centre of the flower. Try to keep the petals at a similar height.

8. Every few petals, grip around the centre of the flower and gently fold out the very tops of the petals. This will help to start form the bloom of the carnation.

9. Once all of the petals are attached, tweak and pull out the tops of the petals until you are happy with the carnation. Wrap floristry crepe tape around the stem to cover it completely.

10.

11.
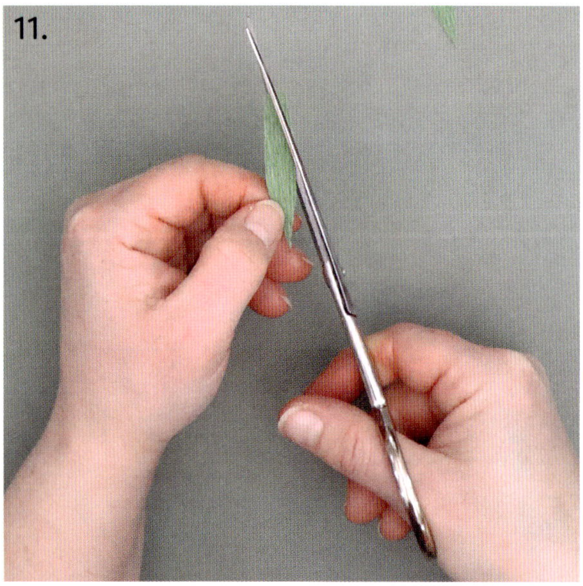

12.

Leaves

10. Cut two rectangles from the green floristry crepe paper ⅜in (10mm) wide and 2in (50mm) long.

11. Cut the rectangles to turn them into long elongated almond shapes for carnation leaves.

12. Attach the leaves to the stem 1½–2in (40–50mm) down from the flower head, securing them in place with the floristry crepe tape. And you have finished – a lovely carnation!

Wild Primrose

Primula vulgaris

On woodland walks, among the grassy verges, you know spring is on its way when a flurry of wild primroses appear. This project shows you how to make a lovely paper flower, which you can put into a flowerpot. Alternatively, you can make a few stems to arrange in a small posy vase.

Materials

- Pale yellow floristry crepe paper (for the petals)
- Yellow or pale orange floristry crepe paper (for the base of the petals)
- White or yellow ⅛in (4mm) paper straw
- Paper-covered floristry wire, roughly 16 gauge
- Green floristry crepe paper (for the leaves), ideally in a fine weight (to make it easier to achieve a multilayered texture), but any green crepe paper will work
- Dark green floristry crepe tape
- Hot glue

Tools

- Paper scissors
- Wire cutters
- Glue gun
- Ruler (optional)
- Pencil (optional)

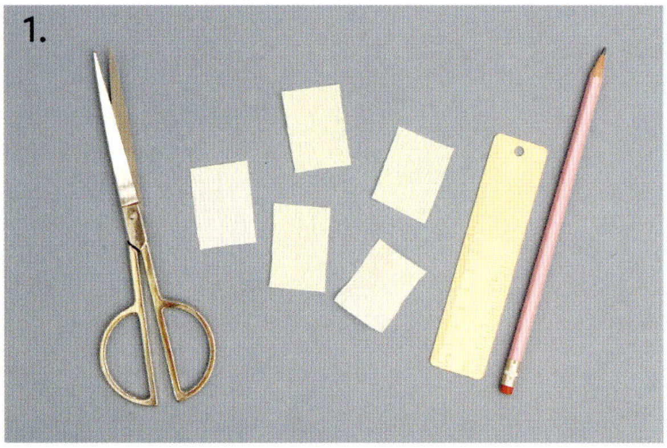
1.

2.

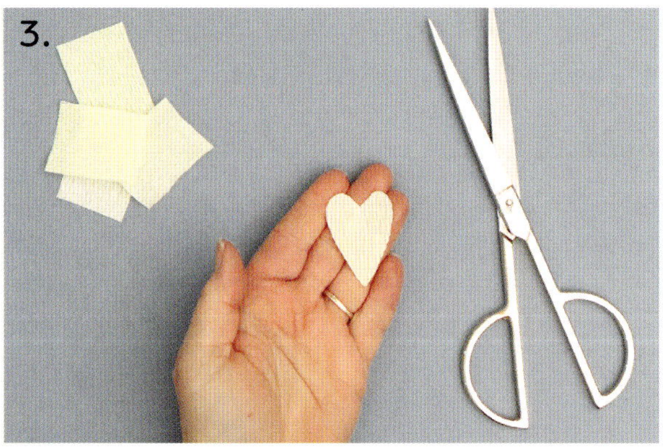
3.

4.

5.

6.

7.

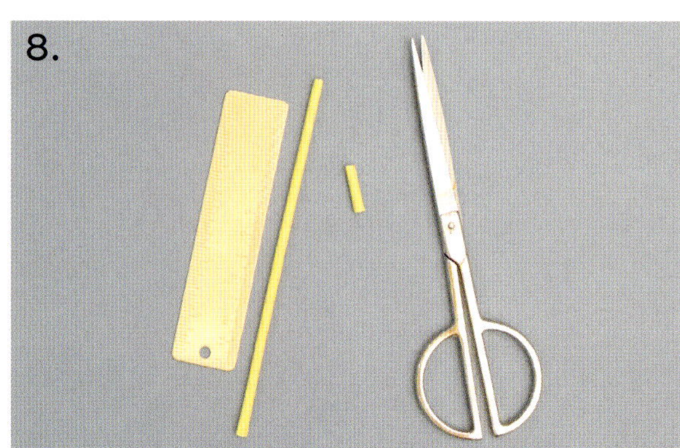
8.

9.

10.

11.

12.

1. From the pale yellow floristry crepe paper, cut five rectangles 1⅛in (30mm) wide and 1½in (40mm) long. The grain of the paper should run up the height of the rectangle.

2. Next, create heart-shaped petals. Fold one of the rectangles in half widthways. The rectangle should now be $\frac{9}{16}$in (15mm) wide and 1½in (40mm) long. Starting at the base of the folded edge, cut diagonally upwards before curving at the top to create a half-heart shape.

3. When you fold the paper back out, you will have a symmetrical heart.

4. Repeat with the other rectangles.

5. From the pale orange or yellow crepe paper, cut five small rectangles ¼in (5mm) wide and ¾in (20mm) long.

6. Cut a curve in the top of each one of these.

7. Using hot glue, attach each curved rectangle centred at the base of the heart. Some of the pale orange will go slightly over the edge of the heart, but don't worry about this. Set aside.

8. Next, cut a ¾–1⅛in (20–30mm) piece from the paper straw.

9. Now add a dot of hot glue to the tip of the paper-covered stem wire. Place the cut straw piece on the tip with the stem wire just inside. Keep the wire fairly near the base of the straw so it can't be seen easily from the top.

10. Glue the heart petals around the straw, keeping them evenly at roughly the same height.

11. Keep going until all of the petals are attached.

12. Use floristry crepe tape to secure the back of the flower and conceal the base of the petals. Wrap the tape around the stem to completely cover it.

13.

14.

15.

16.

17.

18.

19.

20.

21.

22.

Leaves

13. For each leaf, cut a rectangle from the green floristry crepe paper and 2in (50mm) wide and 2¾in (70mm) long.

14. Cut five or six evenly sized strips along the height of the rectangle, but across its grain.

15. Glue these strips back together, slightly overlapping each one.

16. Once all the strips are glued back together, cut a diagonal line through them to create two triangles.

17. Turn one of the triangles over – the grain should now meet in the middle. Ensure the grain runs downwards into a 'V' shape with the point at the base and not as an upside down 'V'.

18. Glue these two triangles together, slightly overlapping each other.

19. Now shape the leaf, using the central meeting point as the main spine of the leaf. Keep the leaf wide with a curved tip.

Assemble

20. To assemble, first use floristry crepe tape to connect several flowers together at the base of their stems, then attach the leaves around the stems using hot glue to secure them.

21. If you are creating a fully potted version of the wild primrose, you will need to create leaves in a variety of sizes. As a guide, you can follow the sizes given below, but the measurements aren't necessarily important – as long as you have a mix of small, medium and large.

    One: 2⅜in (60mm) long and 1½in (40mm) wide
    Three: 2¾in (70mm) long and 2in (50mm) wide
    Two: 3⅛in (80mm) long and 2in (50mm) wide
    One: 4¾in (120mm) long and 3⅛in (80mm) wide
    One: 5½in (140mm) long and 3½in (90mm) wide

22. To put the primrose into a flowerpot, add some brown paper underneath to support the stems. Or, alternatively, don't connect the flowers. Use in a vase, in a buttonhole or however you like!

Dandelion

Taraxacum officinale

These gloriously golden 'weeds' are such beautiful and delicate little flowers. While I am constantly digging up these ferociously avid plants from our garden, I do actually love a little vase full of their sunny petals and unusual leaves. And these paper versions are no different! They are simple to create and very effective for use in buttonholes or for adding to small posies.

Materials

- Yellow floristry crepe paper (for the petals)
- Green floristry crepe paper (for the sepal and leaves)
- Paper-covered floristry wire, roughly 16 gauge
- Dark green floristry crepe tape
- Hot glue

Tools

- Paper scissors
- Wire cutters
- Glue gun
- Ruler (optional)
- Pencil (optional)

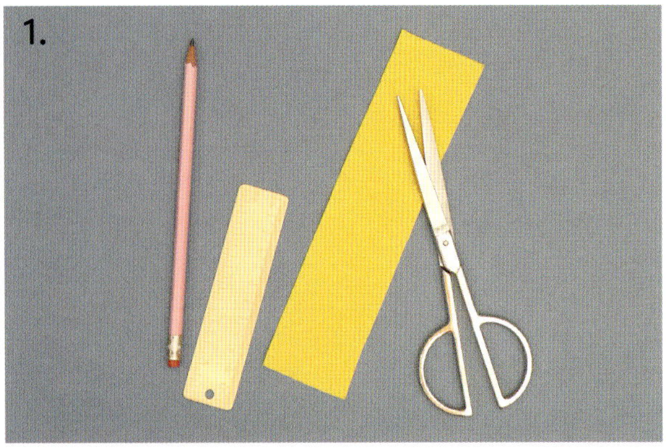
1.

2.

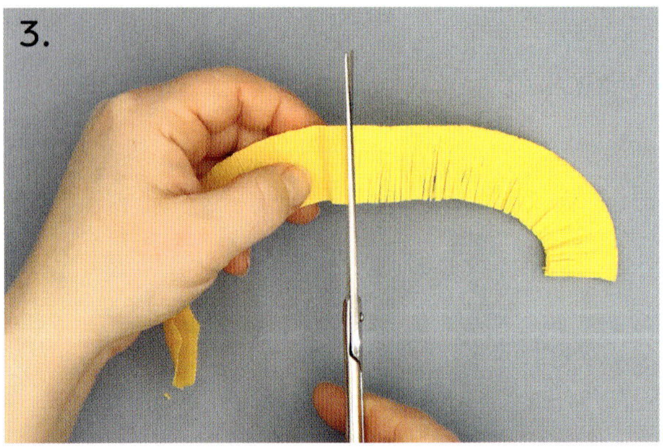
3.

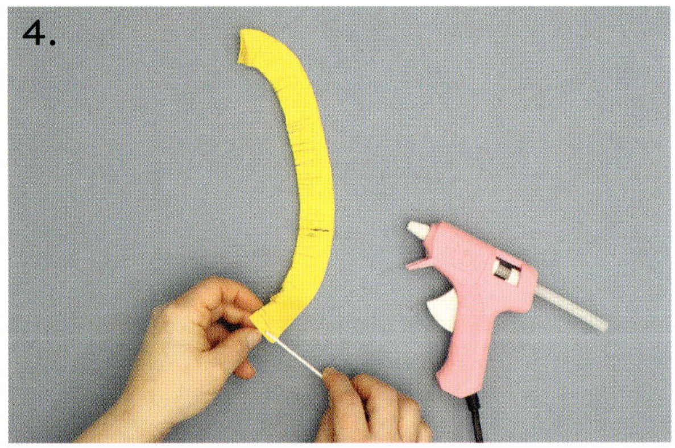
4.

5.

6.

7.

8.

9.

10.

11.

12.

1. Cut a rectangle from the yellow floristry crepe paper 2in (50mm) wide and 8in (200mm) long. The grain should run along the width of the rectangle.

2. Fold it in half widthways, so it is now 1in (25mm) wide and 8in (200mm) long.

3. On the open side, cut into both layers in 5⁄64–⅛in (2–3mm) increments to create a frilled effect. Take care you don't cut all the way through, leaving a small uncut band at the bottom to hold everything together.

4. Place the paper-covered floristry stem wire roughly one-third of the way in at one end of the frilled rectangle and secure it with hot glue.

5. Wind the frilled rectangle around the stem wire, gluing to secure it as you go.

6. Next, cut two rectangles from the green floristry crepe paper 1⅛in (30mm) wide and 1½in (40mm) long. The grain of the paper should run along the width of the rectangle.

7. Cut long, thin zigzags into the rectangle across its width, leaving a band at the bottom. You will have 8–10 triangles, depending on how narrow you cut them.

8. Glue one of these rectangles around the yellow centre so that the tips of the green triangles are just slightly further down from the top.

9. Glue the second green zigzag rectangle around the centre, but this time placing it slightly further down the stem.

10. Grip any excess green floristry crepe paper that is near the stem, before covering and securing it with the floristry crepe tape. Wrap the tape completely around the stem wire to cover it.

11. Fold the second, lower layer of triangles outwards so they curve slightly downwards.

12. Now tease the yellow petals outwards to reveal the dandelion shape!

13.

14.

15.

16.

17.

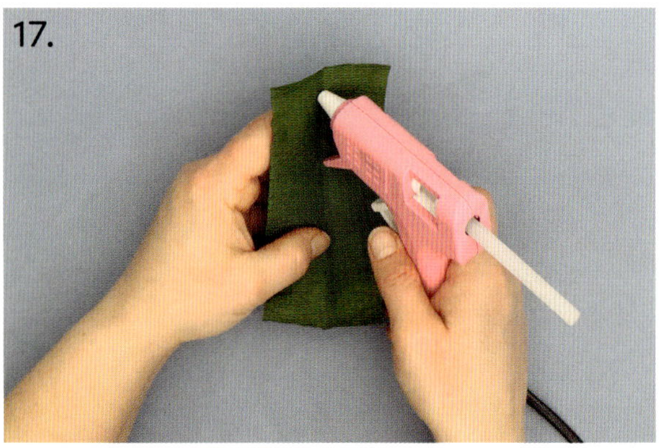

18.

19.

20.

21.

13. You may find at this stage that some of the petals are slightly longer than the others. Trim these back if needed to ensure all the petals are roughly the same length.

Leaves

14. For each leaf, cut a 2⅜in (60mm) square from the green floristry crepe paper.

15. Fully stretch the crepe paper out so it is super thin and is now a rectangle.

16. Fold it in half widthways so it will be a folded rectangle 1⅛in (30mm) wide, then crease.

17. Open the rectangle back out and add a thin line of glue down this crease.

18. Before the glue dries, fold it back closed again – this will create a natural-looking central ridge that will form the spine of the leaf.

19. Now shape the leaf. Dandelion leaves are such unusual shapes! I find it easier to cut with the rectangle still folded together to ensure a symmetrical look at either side. With the folded spine on the left, start cutting at the bottom and work your way upwards, making a series of curved triangles in and out along the length.

20. At the top, curve the cut upwards for a much larger curved triangle.

21. Open the leaf outwards and crease at the centre to mould the leaf flat. You can curve the leaf slightly if you like.

BUD
For a slightly more enclosed dandelion, start with a yellow rectangle 2in (50mm) wide and 8in (200mm) long and do not fold in half. Frill it and assemble in the same way. Don't pull the petals outwards as much as the main in bloom flower.

Poinsettia

Euphorbia pulcherrima

The arrival of a poinsettia in my childhood home always signalled one thing: Christmas was coming. Originally from Mexico, with its traditionally red and green foliage, the poinsettia feels incredibly festive. This make would be lovely as part of the decor on a Christmas table, plus it is the perfect seasonal gift. However, it can adorn the home all year round! This poinsettia project easily comes together with some effective crafty tricks utilizing the grain of the crepe paper for texture.

Materials

- Red floristry crepe paper (for the petals)
- Dark green floristry crepe paper (for the leaves)
- Lime or pale green floristry crepe paper (for the centre)
- Paper-covered floristry wire, roughly 16 gauge
- Floristry stub wire, roughly 20 gauge
- Dark green floristry crepe tape
- Hot glue

Tools

- Paper scissors
- Wire cutters
- Red felt-tip pen (optional)
- Glue gun
- Ruler (optional)
- Pencil (optional)

NOTE: while the classic poinsettia uses the traditional reds and greens, there are hybrid varieties that feature pinks, limes and creams. You can experiment to create a fresh look on this classic and iconic flower.

1.

2.

3.

4.

5.

6.

7.

8.

9.

10.

11.

12.

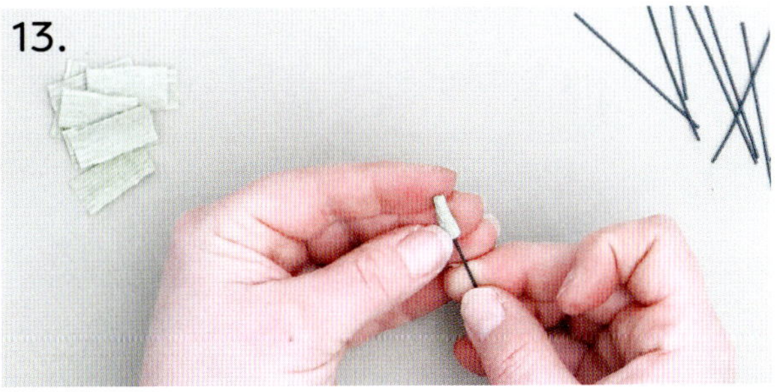

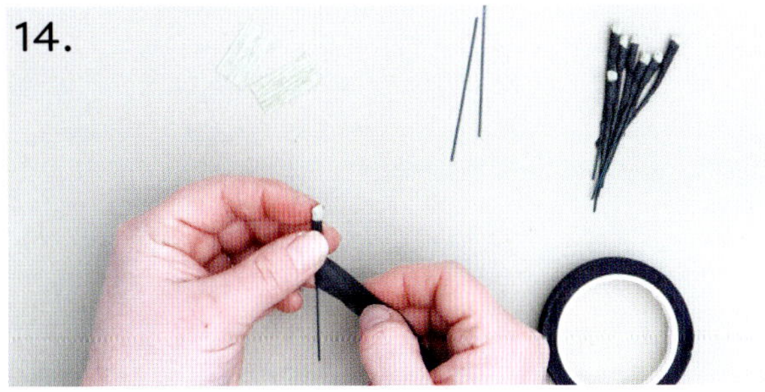

1. The poinsettia 'petals' are, in fact, a form of leaves called bracts (they are called petals in this book). There is no exact format for how many different-sized petals are in a poinsettia, but you can use the following measurements as a guide. Feel free to adapt them if required. Cut the following from the red floristy crepe paper:

   Seven large squares: 3⅛–4in (80–100mm)
   Five medium squares: 1½–2⅜in (40–60mm)
   Six small squares: 1⅛–1½in (30–40mm)

2. Cut one of these squares diagonally so you have two triangles. Turn one of the triangles over – the grain should now meet in the middle.

3. Cut a piece of stub wire 1⅛–1½in (30–40mm) longer than the triangle diagonal length. The additional length of wire will be used to attach to the central stem later.

4. Ensure the grain of the two triangles runs downwards into a 'V' shape with the point at the bottom (and not as an upside down 'V'). This is important to ensure there is a consistent natural texture in the petals, and later the same with the leaves. Run a small amount of hot glue along the diagonal edge of one of the triangles, then add the stub wire on top. Place the tip of the wire at the top of the triangle, with 1½in (40mm) of the other end extending beyond the triangle.

5. Add a second line of hot glue on top of the stub wire (only where it is on the crepe paper, not down the full length), before placing the other triangle on top, just slightly overlapping the first triangle.

6. Now cut into the paper at one side to start creating a poinsettia petal shape. Start off narrow at the bottom, curving widely at the sides, before going back down into a narrow point at the top. Be careful not to cut into the wire as this could damage the scissors. If you need to trim around the wire, use wire cutters. Repeat back down the other side to make a mirror image of the shape.

7. Once you are happy with the petal shape, bend the wire inside into a slight curve. Poinsettia petals are often quite undulating in appearance.

8. Repeat steps 3–7 for the remaining red petals.

9. Use the green floristry crepe for leaves. You can add as many or as few leaves as you would like – I have made three leaves in the same way as the petals, starting with rectangles 3⅛in (80mm) wide and 4¾ (120mm) long.

10. To make the central pistil section, cut 10 pieces of floristry stub wire, each roughly 1½in (40mm) long. Did you know that it is this small central part that is the actual flower of a poinsettia?

11. Cut 10 small rectangles of lime or pale green crepe paper, each one ⅜in (10mm) wide and ¾in (20mm) long. The grain of the crepe should run up the height of each rectangle.

12. Place one of the 1½in (40mm) stub wire pieces halfway up one of the rectangles at one end.

13. Roll the paper around the wire, before folding the top downwards so the wire is completely concealed inside.

14. Secure this paper into position on the wire using floristry crepe tape, leaving only the very tip of crepe paper exposed above the tape. Repeat with the remaining nine stub wires and rectangles.

15.

16.

17.

18.

19.

20.

21.

22.

15. As an optional step, slightly add colour to some of the tips with a small dot of a red felt-tip pen. I have done this on six out of 10 pistils to replicate the natural appearance of a poinsettia centre.

16. Next, attach each of these 10 central pieces to the stem wire, forming in a cluster around it. Place each one ¾–1⅛in (20–30mm) above the wire tip so that it is hidden inside, but they don't need to be perfectly level. Use floristry crepe tape to securely attach a few at a time.

17. Now attach the petals, starting with the smallest petal. Try to make the base of each petal level with the bottom of the central pistil section. Use floristry crepe tape to secure the stub wire to the central stem wire. Try to leave a small gap between the pistil section and the base of the petals. This is often how the real poinsettia is structured.

18. Move around the central stem as you attach the petals. You could mix up where you attach the medium and larger petals as they are often not evenly distributed, so don't feel it needs to be perfectly balanced.

19. Keep attaching petals around the central stem using plenty of floristry crepe tape to ensure everything is really secure.

20. Once all the petals are attached, move on to adding in the leaves underneath the petals in the same way.

21. Wrap the floral crepe tape around the stem wire to completely cover it.

22. Once everything is attached, bend and move the wire in the petals into position if required.

Holly

Ilex aquifolium

This is iconic winter foliage in classic Christmas colours. Those deep and dark green glossy leaves against the pop of red berry jewels make for a striking look. Parts of this holly project take a bit of forward planning, but I can promise it is totally worth it – the small extra touches really elevate the make. This project can be made with or without the berries, but either way the holly would be lovely incorporated into a garland, wreath or nestled into a winter bouquet.

Materials

For the leaves

- Dark green cardstock, 150gsm or less (for the leaves)
- Thin green floristry stub wire, roughly 22 gauge
- Paper-covered floristry wire, roughly 16 gauge
- Brown floristry crepe tape
- PVA glue
- Hot glue

For the berries

- White air-dry clay
- Thin green floristry stub wire, roughly 22 gauge
- Red nail varnish or paint

Tools

- Paintbrush
- Paper scissors
- Wire cutters
- Glue gun
- Polystyrene, foam or similar (optional)
- Ruler (optional)
- Pencil (optional)

1.

2.

3.

4.

5.

6.

7.

8.

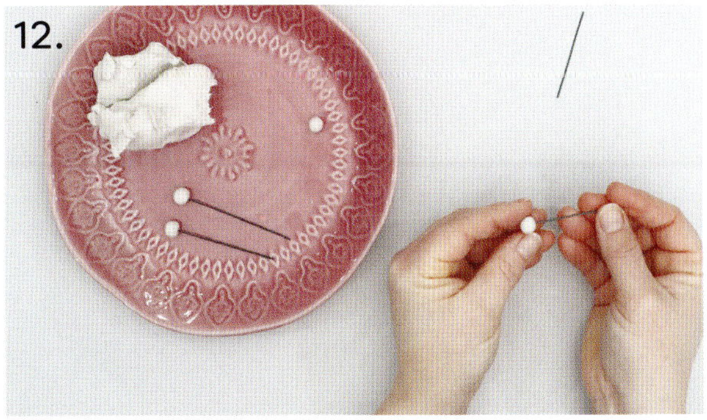

Leaves

1. Use a paintbrush to lightly coat the green cardstock in PVA glue all over. Leave to dry. This will provide that luscious and glossy look for the holly leaves.

2. Once dry, cut rectangles 2¾–3⅛in (70–80mm) long and 2–2⅜in (50–60mm) wide. You will need one rectangle per leaf. The rectangles may seem wide for leaves, but once assembled, the width will be reduced, making it important to follow these measurements. However, leaves can vary in length and size so feel free to experiment.

3. Fold the rectangle in half widthways to make a clear central crease, then open it back out again.

4. Cut several small arcs into each side of the leaf, making a narrow point at both the top and bottom. The sides do not need to be symmetrical.

5. Add a thin line of hot glue down the central crease on roughly three-quarters of the leaf.

6. Quickly, before the hot glue dries, add a piece of the thin stub wire down the centre, snipped if required so there is roughly 1½in (40mm) extra beyond the leaf. Fold the leaf in half around the wire to glue into position.

7. Open the leaf back out so you now have a central spine in the leaf with the wire enclosed inside.

8. Slightly bend the wire inside the holly leaf so it becomes curved. Crease the leaf slightly to add character.

9. Repeat steps 5–8 for the remaining holly leaves.

Berries

10. Roll the air-dry clay between your palms into small ¼in (5mm) balls. Make as many as you think you may need for the project. You may wish to use gloves as clay can get messy!

11. Cut a 1⅛–1½in (30–40mm) piece of the stub wire for each berry.

12. Push the tip of a wire gently into a clay berry, roughly halfway through. Leave them to dry in a room temperature environment for 24–48 hours.

13.

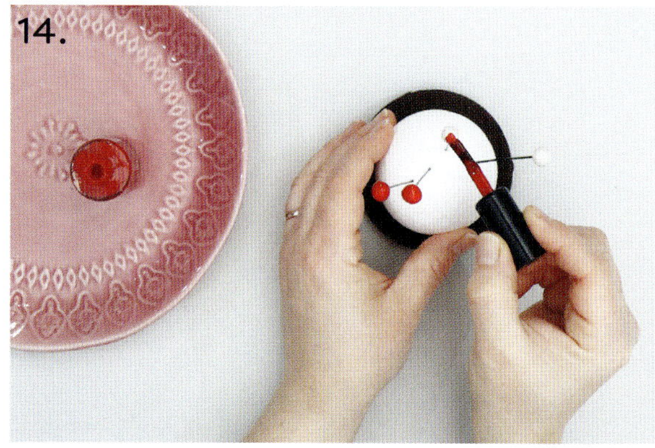
14.

15.

16.

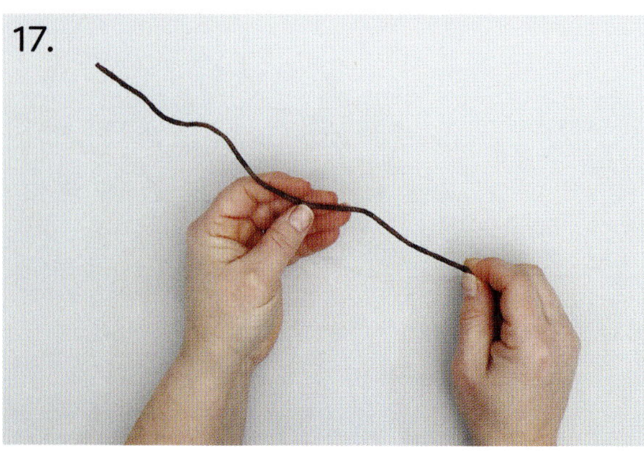
17.

18.

19.

20.

13. Once dry, prop the free ends of the wires with the berries in the polystyrene, foam or something similar – you just need something to hold the berries upright without touching anything while you paint them and they dry. I use a polystyrene sphere balanced in a crepe tape roll simply as that is what I have in my studio – you can use another form of packaging or whatever you have to hand.

14. Paint the berry with the nail varnish or red paint. Red nail varnish is the perfect 'paint' for the berries. It is often available in real berry shades, and it has a wonderful slight enamel sheen to it.

15. Once dry, we are ready to assemble the holly sprig.

16. Wrap brown crepe tape completely around the main floristry stem wire.

17. Slightly curve the stem in places to make it not so straight and more natural looking.

18. Attach each leaf to the brown stem wire, using the brown crepe tape. Try to stagger the leaves roughly ⅜in (10mm) apart. Holly leaves go out in all directions from the main stem, so try to vary their directions.

19. If you are attaching berries, do so in the same way, but sometimes berries are more clustered in place. Make sure to still slightly stagger the berries and leaves, otherwise you can end up with too much stub wire against the stem making it too thick and unrealistic.

20. Keep going with the berries and leaves for as long as you require to make the sprig. And you are finished!

ADDING BERRIES

While you can get sprigs of holly leaves with or without berries, the berries really add a pop of colour to the holly creation. There are many ways to create berries - from purchasing premade berry picks, to using beads, paper balls or felt. However, after experimenting with various techniques, these are consistently the strongest and most 'berry' looking in appearance! While you need to prep some of this in advance, if you are making a project that you know will include berries, why not make a huge batch of them, ready to add into garlands, wreaths and Christmas decorations.

Foliage

Emerald Palm

Ruscus

By including foliage in the floral designs, you can really add depth and interest to the overall look. You can choose either standard paper or floristry crepe paper to make leaves, but the grain of the crepe paper adds texture to their surface – such as in the emerald palm make. You can adapt the techniques to make ruscus and, in fact, most leaves can be assembled in the same way. Feel free to experiment with the sizes and shapes of the leaves to create any foliage you would like.

Materials

- Green floristry crepe paper
- Paper-covered floristry wire, roughly 16 gauge
- Green floristry crepe tape

Tools

- Paper scissors
- Wire cutters
- Ruler (optional)
- Pencil (optional)

1.
2.
3.
4.
5.
6.
7.
8.

9.

Emerald Palm

1. Start by cutting strips roughly 1⅛in (30mm) wide along the green floristry crepe paper roll. The grain of the paper should run up the height of the strips.

2. You will need 26 leaves in total, the longest being 6in (150mm) in length, and the shortest 3½in (90mm). Start by cutting two 1⅛in (30mm) wide rectangles in each of the following lengths:

6in (150mm)	5⅛in (130mm)	4¼in (110mm)
5¾in (145mm)	5in (125mm)	4⅛in (105mm)
5½in(140mm)	4¾in (120mm)	4in (100mm)
5¼in (135mm)	4½in (115mm)	3¾in (95mm)
		3½in (90mm)

These leaves will gently stagger down in length by reducing them by roughly ¼in (5mm) each time.

3. To shape each leaf, start with a narrow base, cut towards the side in a wide curved shape, before coming to a point at the top and making it almost symmetrical down the other side.

4. As you cut them, try to keep the leaves laid out by size order to make it easier to attach them.

5. Starting with the two shortest leaves, secure into place at the top of the stem wire using the floristry crepe tape. Try to secure the small base of the leaf to the side of the stem and alternate the side on which you attach each one. Try not to use too much tape – otherwise the central stem will become too thick.

6. Moving down the stem, attach the remaining leaves from smallest to largest, slightly staggered apart, evenly on either side of the wire, using the tape to secure them.

7. Keep going until all of the leaves are attached.

8. Cover the rest of the stem by wrapping it in the tape.

9. Depending on how far apart you place the leaves, their arrangement will change how the palm appears.

1.

2.

3.

4.

5.

6.

Ruscus

You can adapt the emerald palm (see pages 152–153) by cutting any size or shape of leaves, before attaching them to a central stem. You can also use the same materials as the emerald palm, but here I have switched to a darker shade of green, and a lighter weight crepe paper. Additionally, make the central stem from thin green floristry stub wire, roughly 22 gauge.

1. Start by cutting 10 rectangles 1½in (40mm) wide and 3⅛in (80mm) long. Keep the grain running along the length of the rectangles. You can cut more leaves if you would like the sprig to be larger.

2. Shape the leaves and attach in the same way as for the emerald palm.

3. If you prefer, you can attach each leaf to an individual wire stem instead of directly to a central stem.

4. Use stub wire to attach small lengths to individual leaves. Wrap the stub wire stems in the floristry crepe tape, before attaching these to the main stem.

5. You can experiment by joining sprigs together to make multi-stem varieties. How you join the leaves to the central stem (with individual wire stems or not) can really vary how the foliage looks. Multiple sprigs grouped together can be very effective.

Eucalyptus

Eucalyptus

Indigenous to Australia, eucalyptus is a great foliage that will add interest to any mixed bouquet. Or, with its striking architectural form, a pure bunch of these leaves will make a stunning statement! Try to find shades of green with a bluey tinge to them, but otherwise any green cardstock can be transformed into these simple but effective sprigs.

Materials

- Green cardstock, A4 (letter) size, 150gsm or less
- Paper-covered floristry wire, roughly 16 gauge
- Green floristry crepe tape

Tools

- Paper scissors
- Wire cutters
- Ruler (optional)
- Pencil (optional)
- Hot glue gun (optional)

1.

2.

3.

4.

5.

6.

7.

8.

9.

1. Start by cutting out squares or rectangles of green cardstock in the following dimensions:

   Two pieces: ¾in (20mm) square
   Four pieces: 1⅛in (30mm) long and ¾in (20mm) wide
   Four pieces: 1½in (40mm) long and 1⅛in (30mm) wide
   Four pieces: 2in (50mm) long and 1½in (40mm) wide

   These are rough sizes – as long as you have some small leaves and move up to larger ones, this make will work.

2. Fold each piece in half. For the rectangles, fold in half with the longest edge being folded over – for example, the 2in (50mm) long and 1½in (40mm) wide rectangle would become 1in (25mm) long and 1½in (40mm) wide. Cut a very small snip into the centre of each leaf on the folded edge, then unfold the paper.

3. Now shape each rectangle into leaves. Starting on the folded edge, cut almost circular or oval shapes – you need to leave a small bit of the folded edge in tact around the small central snip.

4. Now wrap floristry crepe paper around the floristry stem wire to completely cover it.

5. Bend the stem wire slightly into a gently curved angle.

6. Starting with the largest leaf, gently slide the stem through the small snip, placing the leaf at the bottom.

7. Continuing with the largest leaves, and gradually working in size order to the smallest leaves, slide the remaining leaves onto the wire stem.

8. Space the leaves evenly, ¾–1⅛in (20 30mm) apart, and ensure the smallest leaf is at the top of the stem.

9. If needed, re-bend the leaves so they are slightly pointing upwards. Try to keep them facing the same direction. And you are finished!

TIP
You shouldn't need any hot glue to hold the leaves in place because the tension of the paper leaves against the crepe tape should be enough. However, if you find the small snip is too large, you could secure the leaf into place with a small bit of hot glue underneath.

Uses

You can use your paper flowers in almost any way as you would do real flowers. Paper flowers also have the added benefit of not needing any water to keep on thriving! Your paper flowers could be used for big celebrations such as parties, weddings and events, or just because you want a lovely bunch of 'daffs' all year round. If you could guarantee a dry day, they could of course also be displayed outdoors – I would check that weather forecast!

Vases

Your paper flower creations will, of course, look lovely in a vase, but they may need some extra support to keep them in position. When you put real flowers into a vase, they naturally fall into place, and you can quickly arrange them if desired. However, wire stems are much stiffer, and might need some bending or adjusting. If required, you can entwine different wire stems around each other to secure, or tie together using more wire or floristry crepe tape. This is particularly useful if you have made a flower with a shorter stem than is ideal – you can just attach it to another flower to make it appear higher up!

It is also useful to have something like tissue paper or newspaper, bubble wrap or perhaps even fabric to nestle inside vases – you can push your stems into this for extra support too if required. Or, you can use glass beads/stones used for traditional floristry displays. Pour them into your vase before pushing your stems into place. The beads/stones will help to keep your stems in position.

Experiment with different containers to display your flowers in – little posies look lovely grouped together in a cup, mug, jug or perhaps old bottles. You could keep the stems very short and arrange your blooms into a bowl. Or you could even make a paper vase.

Wreaths

Wind your wire stems into wreath bases for all seasons – perhaps you could even mix faux with real dried foliage for an interesting twist on your make. Or, you could hot glue gun everything into position. You would, of course, need to keep your wreath indoors to stop the paper flowers getting soggy, but, wreaths can look beautiful on interior doors, hung up as a piece of art or anywhere you would like to brighten your home.

Garlands

You could combine lots of flowers and foliage into long garlands. Use longer lengths of wire as your main central stem and wrap each flower or leaf around this, building layers together to whatever your desired length. These garlands could be added to the Christmas tree, make a nice central table decoration or entwined amongst a staircase. Traditionally, garlands can also be hung above fireplaces on a mantelpiece – but due to the flammable properties of paper – I would highly recommend not to do this!

Christmas

At Christmas, you could also make full blooms to individually add decorations into the branches of your tree. Wind the wire stems along branches to add a floral element to your traditional Christmas décor! Red roses, classic poinsettia or white lilies would look lovely among the green fir.

Table décor

Single stems or small bunches of flowers look lovely as table displays. Perhaps they could be nestled among a napkin, tucked into place settings, or just several vases grouped together. However, be careful of naked flames.

Buttonholes

Some of these flowers would look lovely made into 'miniature' versions – adjust some of the sizes and mix and match to create little groups of flowers for corsages or buttonholes. You could tie some ribbon around for added décor – and use a simple safety pin to attach to whatever you are wearing for a special occasion.

Hair accessories

Paper flowers would look lovely added to hair clips, bows, or you could create huge floral head bands for festival vibes.

Cake toppers

I often use paper flowers for decorating cakes, these add such a fun and pretty element to your baking creations. Use cocktail sticks or wooden skewers as the stems, or ensure whatever you push into your cake is food safe and clean. However if your paper flowers come into contact with icing, they may soak up oil and/or colourings; the flowers may not be resuable for more than one occasion. And again, be careful of those candles!

Giftwrap

If I have wrapped a gift and tied it up with a bow, I sometimes nestle a little paper flower just under the bow. Your present will look lovely, and your recipient gets an additional gift – a handmade bloom to treasure!

Petal and Leaf Shapes

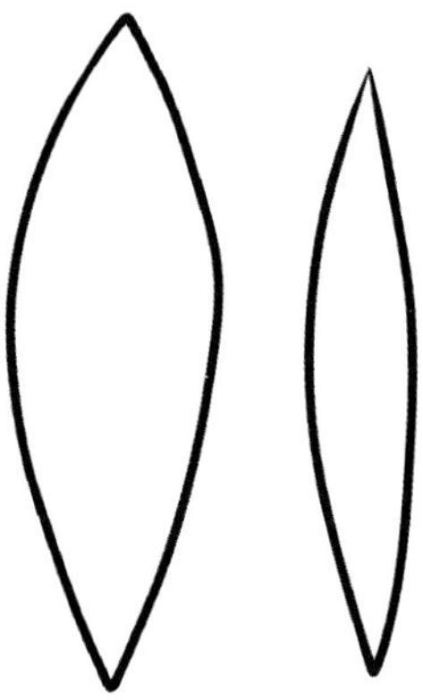

Almond

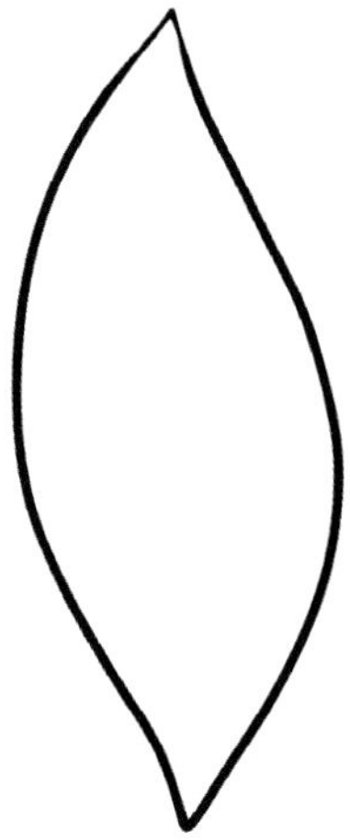

Leaf

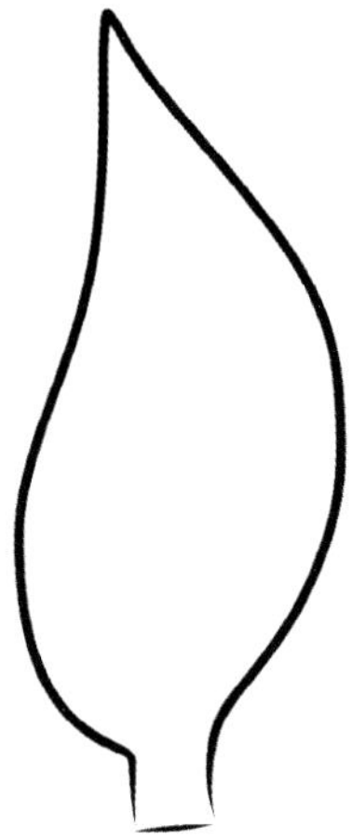

Leaf with base

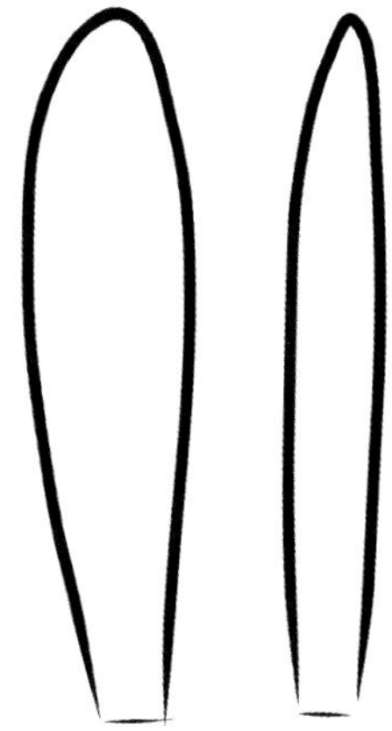

Daisy style

Hot-air balloon

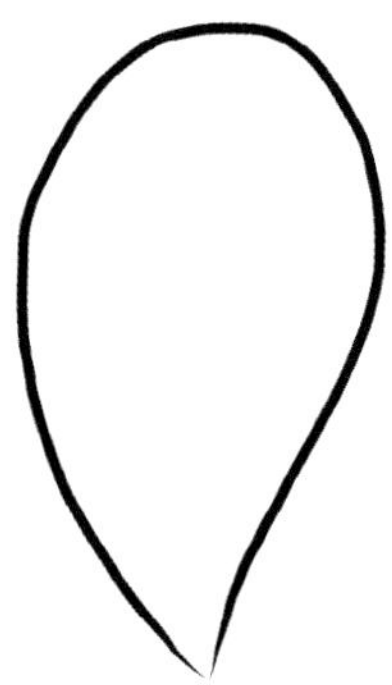

Teardrop

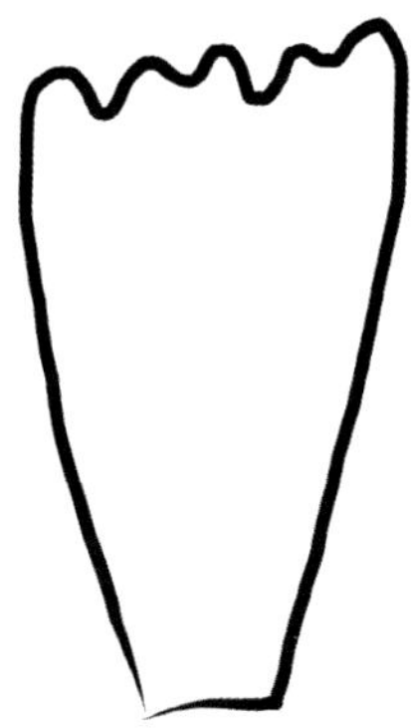

Carnation & French marigold style

Eucalyptus

Heart

Heart with base

Wide heart

Resources

Materials

Hobbycraft
www.hobbycraft.co.uk

Canford Daler Rowney
www.daler-rowney.com

Floristry Warehouse
www.floristrywarehouse.com

Amazon
www.amazon.co.uk

The Homemakery
www.thehomemakery.co.uk

Fred Aldous
www.fredaldous.co.uk

Little Crafty Bugs
www.littlecraftybugs.co.uk

Scissors

Katie Leamon
www.katieleamon.com

Acknowledgements

This book is dedicated to:

My Mum and Dad – Anne and Mike – who have been my absolutely avid supporters since day one. Thank you for everything you do and always listening. This will be a big deal to both of you too! Keep your chin up – or you won't see your horizons.

To my husband Dan, my Lad, who I simply could not be without. Thank you for your incredibly continuous support, and for putting up with craft, paper and petals all over our house...

To my dear boys – Freddie and Rupert, my own 'Petal' and 'Pip' – you have put up with me forever crafting and making flowers by your side. I am grateful for your beautiful, unconditional love and understanding – thank you for letting Mummy pursue her crafty dream.

Hayley, Jenny, Laura, Louise, Heather – thank you for being my continuous cheerleaders. Heather – YNCTAM (You Never Cease To Amaze Me!). And, to ALL of my friends and family who pushed me to launch 'The Crafty Lass' in the first place, and have been with me ever since!

Thank you to Jo Horne for allowing me into your beautiful Grey Barn home to take photographs. Your help, flexibility and stunning location has brought absolute joy.

Thank you to Stuart Hillard – we were both meant to be there that day; that conversation was meant to happen. Huge thank you to Jonathan Bailey, for both reading my email all those years ago, and then subsequently making me cry when you called to tell me this was finally happening! And finally, thank you to all the team at GMC for trusting me to write a book. Wow, I WROTE A BOOK!

Thank you Jenny Stewart for your unwavering patience in creating the 'perfect' author profile photo, surrounded by my flowers!

"Luck is when preparation meets opportunity" – *Roman philosopher Seneca*

First published 2024 by
GMC Publications Ltd,
Castle Place, 166 High Street,
Lewes, East Sussex, BN7 1XU, UK.

ISBN 978-1-78494-688-3

A catalogue record for this book is available from the British Library.

PUBLISHER Jonathan Bailey
PRODUCTION Jim Bulley
SENIOR PROJECT EDITOR Susie Behar
DESIGNER Emily Hurlock
PHOTOGRAPHY Paula Milner
COLOUR ORIGINATION GMC Reprographics
Printed and bound in China
The Crafty Lass® is a Registered Trademark

To order a book, contact:

GMC Publications Ltd
Castle Place, 166 High Street,
Lewes, East Sussex, BN7 1XU
United Kingdom
Tel: +44 (0)1273 488005
www.gmcbooks.com